The ASSERTIVE PARENT

The ASSERTIVE PARENT

Hacks, Traps & Strategies for Raising Authentic Teens

ADVOCATE, MENTOR, COACH
Daniel Patterson

Wyatt-MacKenzie Publishing
DEADWOOD, OREGON

The Assertive Parent
Hacks, Traps & Strategies for Raising Authentic Teens

Daniel Patterson

ISBN: 978-1-942545965
Library of Congress Control Number: 2018943437

Wyatt-MacKenzie Publishing
DEADWOOD, OREGON

Wyatt-MacKenzie Publishing, Inc.
info@wyattmackenzie.com

Dedicated to my wife & children; I love you!

Written in memory of Len.

Contents

Introduction

Authenticity is a tired and dying breed. And it's in trouble. Conformity is in; going with the grain is standard; and both strategies, in the short term at least, can appear to be significantly easier than swimming upstream. As such, it's difficult to parent or teen according to how one's true internal compass might independently dictate. Upstream is exhaustive, pays little return on that investment in the short term, and can often result in isolative or seemingly lonely moments in time. What's more, downstream is sexy. This mainstream current propels *the here and now*; it roars with excitement and rapids, eventually dumping its passengers to a destination void of long-term thinking, and where absence of accountability prevails.

Undeniably, maintaining an authentic self, either as a teenager or a parent, is less photo-friendly than the alternative. It's riddled with annoyances like structure, long-term pragmatics and moderation. The contrast between those gliding downstream and those pushing up it isn't readily or easily identifiable. In fact, many people do an amazing job faking their outward appearance and seemingly convince even themselves that they are making decisions true to their own internal compass.

Imitation-grade authenticity is rampant. You can find it frequently packaged as individuality and independent thought. Again, this is evident both with children and adults alike, as the generations morph into one sub-culture. In many affluent communities, as well as all over pop culture media, high school is the new college. Teenage lifestyle options and expectations have accelerated tremendously. Young teens find themselves running at an ever-increasing clip. This clip soon becomes a full-fledged sprint. And typically, thereafter the velocity of this sprint transitions into the dangerous warp-speed lifestyle of a college student. Now this isn't to say college isn't a place to push the envelope. It often is. I did. But there exists an inevitable danger zone when youthful kids begin experiencing the temptation, recreation and responsibility that accompanies this phase of life at fifteen years old. Now can we stop teens from experimentation? Probably not. Can we prevent them from exposure to said landmines? No way. But we can *adult* with more clarity, more morality and minimize our own contribution to, and responsibility for, such experiences.

To every ying, there is yang. In the spirit of the metaphor, it's important to recognize that teens (the ying) are not the only ones being pulled out of their *age-appropriate*, or *life experience-appropriate* phase in their life. Parents, too (the yang), are facing similar temptation to defy their most natural age and stage, only they are fighting gravity in the opposite direction: seeking to be young again. As the teens are on-ramping onto the College Expressway, there is a line of should-be adults exiting their own expressway to grab a bite to eat (or a beer to shotgun) on the Teenage Glory Days Parkway. There exists a significant undercurrent, riptide (or whatever you want to call it) pulling many should-be adults and parents within our communities, back in time. In apparent or implied defiance to time (and their requisite ages and stages of life) the should-be adults and parents haphazardly abandon their appropriate vantage points, and choose instead to live vicariously through the next generation. This age-and-stage-abandonment is passively at best, and more often actively, employed by enabling teenagers and their overly and prematurely accelerated college-and-beyond lifestyle. What does this look like? As opposed to knowing that teenagers will at some point experience things like getting drunk, high, having sex, or the similar, and trying to make these experiences harder to experience and process lesson free, these wrong-way adult should-be drivers on the Age-and-Stage-Appropriate Express-way instead foster such experiences with celebratory and *they're going to do it anyway* expressions of rationality. We know what happens to wrong-way drivers. It's great on an empty road. But on the busy roads of life, it will lead to nothing short of a head-on collision.

The Assertive Parent is a mix of practical and reality-based tools and strategies that I have developed and successfully implemented with teenagers and parents over the past fifteen years. These various tools were practically driven from inevitable trial and error cycle of working in the trenches alongside teenagers and their parents through almost every imaginable scenario. This book will help you maximize your fight in the war on peaking in high school; for in many ways, peaking in high school can lead to a life of being known as the angry drunk in your hometown, stuck living in a world of *what was* and *what could-have-beens.* The primary mission of this book is to open your eyes to the fact that more than ever, parents are fostering an environment where high school is the new college, and failure to launch or failure to stay launched is status quo. *Assertive Parenting* is your survival guide for the messy world of teenagers and the adulting that is required to properly guide these hormonal, intellectual, creative, often unmotivated, and authenticity-seeking creatures into the next season of their lives.

Parenting teenagers is a crazy process that requires a bob-and-weave mentality—in certain situations you will find yourself ruling with an iron-fisted *my house, my rules* paradigm, while other times you will find yourself plugging holes on the walls of the Titanic with a passive *this is impossible* mindset. Both of those approaches, extreme in their own way, represent the markers that we should strive to stay within—goal posts on the field of parenting. I'm not suggesting that parents should let their kids run around in a Montessori-gone-wild frenzy where they must be overly in touch with their feelings, guide every aspect of their learning or be treated like an adult. I am also not suggesting that they are locked up and never let out of the house in fear that they'll see porn on someone's phone or snag a beer from a neighbor's refrigerator. To develop an authentic teen, we must parent from the middle, with balance, and a combination of a firm hand and a big heart. If nothing else, this book will raise your awareness of your own parenting paradigm and force you to decide how active, or passive you need to become [or remain] to be the best parent possible.

It's my observation that 90% of teen behaviors have only 10% to do with conscious choice or thought of those teenagers. Of course, my observation is based on experience and has no scientific research to support it. Still, I'd say it's 99% accurate. In fact, the 90% percentile of the teen behaviors mentioned have 100% to do with the adults in their lives. Now if you're like most readers, your mind went straight to negative behaviors. But this 90% also represents the positive behaviors. And it illustrates a point: adults have inherent and undeniable influence over children. And teenagers after all, are children. Just giant ones with crazy attitudes. And while I could draft a nice pie chart to breakdown the various players or stakeholders who make up a typical teenager's adult-influence-infrastructure, I would have to in fact draw a new pie chart for each of my readers. And that would take too many pages. Teenagers become teenagers after years of not being one. And in those formative years their brain is constantly collecting, analyzing and storing the data it collects. Again, I make this claim on purely a practical level, and not whatsoever in the clinical sense; although I imagine that similar scientific claims are widely accepted as fact.

The purpose our time together as you read this book is not to hyper-analyze all the things that teenagers are doing wrong today, and prescribe a formula to follow that will solve those multivariable social-emotional equations. No, this book is meant to show you, my reader, how to become more aware, engaged, and compassionately assert yourself into the landscape of your teens' lives in a more meaningful way. And when I say your teen, that doesn't mean that you must be their parent. They may be on a team you coach, in a classroom you teach, in a school you run, your niece or nephew, godchild, or neighbor you've known since they ran around the house naked. Or they may be the one you birthed. Your teen (whatever that your means), may be in bed fast asleep right now as you read this (unless you haven't taken their phone, because then they're not asleep, they're on it ... go check, I'll be here; give them the gift of a full night's much needed sleep). Or your teen may be pulling an all-nighter from a classic case of *I'll do it later.* Or they may be "sleeping at a friend's house," you sucker. There are endless choices to select from.

Despite all their trepidation, teenagers are never a lost cause. So, to the parents who dismissively think that it's too late to make any impact on their older teen, I urge you to reconsider that assertion. On the contrary, people of all ages are acutely adaptable when they feel compelled to do so. Use employers as an example. Companies implement new policies at work—a dress code, or hours of operation or job duties—and employees adapt. Sure, they no doubt bemoan said changes, and smear their boss with colorful language at happy hour, but they do it. Teachers change policies from school year to school year, and students fall in line. Teenagers are adaptable creatures, and so, too, do the adults in their lives need to be. But teenagers are incredibly stubborn, too. And so, too, do the adults in their lives need to be. And teenagers are incredibly sensitive, loving, and potential positive. To which I say, so are you. You get the point.

I've broken this book into four core parts, with the intention for you to choose your own parent adventure. I recommend you read it once in its entirety to garner the all-encompassing message, look for common themes and content overlap. Participation is essential to full utilization of this book. You'll be asked to think, reflect, challenge your current practices, and anticipate landmines you'd most likely prefer aren't possible. Grab a pen, dig in, and allow this to help you on your journey to becoming a more engaged and assertive parent.

PART ONE

Drugs, Alcohol & Nicotine

Sportscenter monopolizes the TV as Dad takes refuge on the couch. Soon, Mom returns with the youngsters from an early soccer game. The freshman eventually finds her way downstairs to find leftover pancakes. The weekend reprieve. Real life.

Talk turns to evening plans: parents have dinner with friends, there's a sitter for the youngsters, and the freshman ... well, it's unclear. She's going to Kelly's, or Sarah's, unless it's Michelle's; but Kelly and Sarah are fighting, so they'll probably go to Nicole's; she's neutral. Confusion reigns. Names and households are familiar; there's no mention of a party. This well-timed monologue is the first in a series of moves used to clear the way for a night of nomadic partying.

Mom and Dad hardly react; their freshman, while dramatic, is a *good* kid. She gets "A"s, plays varsity sports, teachers love her, she's mostly polite. They trust her, and aren't super interested in the social details, assuming she makes curfew and maintains her resume. She has a cellphone, debit card, and Uber. It's a win-win: parents enjoy their night, youngsters get the babysitter, and the freshman is entertained with no activity required from parents. And just like that, the freshman departs to begin her night of nomadic partying.

Nomads are simultaneously everywhere and nowhere. Social media, smartphones, and youthful scheming allow teens to work with efficiency. They communicate hourly, while their parents don't. This communication-heavy alliance helps them systematically outwit, outplay, and outlast parental oversight. By laying the proper groundwork (equal parts convoluted and convincing), an illusion of the well-monitored night is solidified. Though the quick and obligatory parental call or text was executed, the fluid and subtle nature of their plans escape any tangible oversight from a busy or mildly distracted parent.

On-demand transit is key. The nomadic model utilizes the cover of transit to leverage freedom. These non-driving teens carve increments of unsupervised time into opportunities to inhale cans of light beer and shots of vodka (not in the Uber, but in the moments before and after). Soon-to-be freshmen house-hop on Saturday nights with booze-filled backpacks, as they traverse neighborhood greenbelts. Upon arrival, evidence is hidden as they ride their buzz until the lead nomad signals it's time to refill, or the surprised host's patience wears thin. Uber is beckoned, and they hone in on their next target.

Nomads are good kids. Teens often escape parent accountability because they are considered (and in many ways are) *good* kids. But *good* and *safe* are not the same. In groups teens experience an exponential increase in risk-taking behaviors. This, paired with alcohol, shrinks the *good* while elevating the *reckless*. Too often, the GPA is a dominant consideration in determining social freedoms. More so, the *they're going to do it anyhow* (they will) mentality clouds more assertive parenting strategies. But is this a healthy paradigm from which to parent? As such, the age for acceptability of excessive teenage partying continues to decrease, and now encroaches into the middle school years.

Nomads easily identify the absentee or susceptible parent. The sad truth is that a small minority of parents marginalize the efforts of the more responsible ones. Typically, these parents seek to relive their own teen years through their children, or to increase the popularity of their child. They mistake the in-home party for acceptance or validation, as opposed to the pure manipulation it really is. Teens feed the ego of the susceptible parent with selfies and compliments to solidify access to the venue for future parties.

Party nomads appear quickly and consume relentlessly. A typical scenario follows this general template: teens seek and receive permission to have a few friends over; news goes viral; a full-blown party erupts; parents try to stop the party; teens won't leave; authorities are called and disperses the crowd; teens quickly regroup via social media, group chats, and Uber to their next landing pad.

A final thought. High school does not have to be the new college, but evermore, it is. Teens crave being edgy; when parents let them drink, alcohol no longer satisfies that adolescent need. So, what will? Life in college is a time for adventure, mistakes, growth, and new experiences; let's not rob our teens of the chance to be teenagers.

Defining your perspective: In this chapter we will examine your philosophy and application of that philosophy in terms of how you manage alcohol, drugs, and nicotine.

Substance use is very much a family decision. This is not meant to tell you whether to allow your teenager to consume alcohol or marijuana, or nicotine (although I don't think you should), but intended to examine how it may be affecting your teenager's overall health and capacity. Our goal here is to raise your level of awareness as to your contribution to their use (and their friends' use) of alcohol and marijuana and nicotine.

Parent Alcohol Diagnostic

Directions: Check all that apply to you or your teenager as it relates to alcohol.

☐ I allow its use.

☐ I allow its use in our home.

☐ I allow other teens to use alcohol in my home.

☐ I get permission from parents before serving their teen.

☐ I don't allow alcohol use.

☐ I know they drink, but haven't addressed the issue.

☐ I have clear consequences if it's used.

☐ I have never had an incident with my teen and alcohol.

☐ My teen does not drink.

☐ My teen uses ridesharing apps.

☐ I regularly drop off and pick up my teen from parties.

☐ I allow my teen's friends to stay over if they've been drinking.

☐ I talk to my teen about the dangers of alcohol.

☐ I have no idea if my teen drinks.

☐ I don't want to know if my teen drinks alcohol.

☐ I assume they drink, because I did when I was their age.

☐ I know which families allow teens to drink in their homes.

☐ I would prefer they didn't drink, but I can't stop them.

Unpacking the diagnostic: Take a minute to review your answers—what boxes you checked. I find the act of writing things down, in plain view, free from judgement, is the best way to understand the current state of alcohol within the home. What speaks to you? Is there anything you intentionally skipped? Did you experience any twinges of guilt or shame or embarrassment with this list? Would you show it to your neighbor?

Personal Reflection

Directions: Based on the previous questions, rate yourself on the following sliding scales.

My overall awareness of my teen's drinking is:

○ High

○ Elevated

○ Neutral

○ Low

○ Nonexistent

My overall contribution to their drinking is:

○ High

○ Elevated

○ Neutral

○ Low

○ Nonexistent

My overall concern regarding their use of alcohol is:

○ High

○ Elevated

○ Neutral

○ Low

○ Nonexistent

Knowing where you stand: As stated before, it is important that both you and your teen know your philosophy regarding alcohol and the values that support that philosophy. Teens need consistency; no one wins when one weekend they are permitted to drink, the next they are not; or in one instance there is a consequence from drinking, but in another there is not.

Task: In the chart below, evaluate your stance, position, rules and consequences regarding your teen and alcohol. This is a personal, family decision. This section is not intended to tell you what to do. Rather it is meant to heighten your awareness regarding your philosophy and the values behind it. It is vital to be clear about the rules, expectations, and consequences with your teen.

My philosophy:	My values:
My rules:	**The consequences:**

Alcohol: know where you stand ... and stand there.

☐ I understand my philosophy regarding teens and alcohol

☐ I can articulate the values behind my stance on teen alcohol use.

☐ I have rules in place to appropriately support my philosophy and values.

☐ I have thought through interventions and consequences I might need to use in response to alcohol use or abuse.

Fake IDS: The advent of the internet has been complicit in your teenager's ability to get a well-made, or well-made-enough for shady vendors, fake ID.

Before we get into it ... here are some common parent defensive responses:

✓ I had one as a teen

✓ I'd rather them have it than get a ticket for minor in possession

✓ All their friends have one, so I don't want them to be left out

✓ I can't stop them from having one or getting another—so what's the point

Acquisition: It won't take long for you to search the internet and find a wide variety of options for teenagers to obtain a fake ID. Many of these sites have iron-clad disclaimers that clearly state the products sold are novelty items, leaving little room for parents to take legal action when their teen uses said fake ID in the process of making bad choices, receiving heavy legal consequences, or winding up with alcohol poisoning. Not so long ago a parent I know sent her daughter off to college. This college freshman, like many, brought her new fake ID with her to the bar scene. As a rookie binge-drinker, she ended up in the hospital, alone, and nearly died. When her parents were eventually called, the mother went into full Magnum PI mode, tracing her daughter's fake ID back to the vendor who sold it to her. Turns out the vendor issues 3 IDs as a package, in case one is lost, stolen, or confiscated by parents or authorities. Long story short, Magnum Mama went full legal, only to soon discover that her efforts were futile as her daughter, at 18 years old, had signed her rights away via unread fine print upon purchase.

These sites rip off your teen: If for no other reason, one way that the fake ID market is bad for your teen is financially. I've been told by more than a few teens that they placed orders, paid for them with a debit or credit card, only to have no fake ID arrive. Smart move by the companies selling—what is the teen going to do? Call their mom and say this company took my money?

Hardly. So, often the teen will double or triple pay before their soon-to-be-taken ID arrives. Now this is assuming that the teen has placed their own order, using their own credit or debit card.

But I watch their money: Of course, you watch their money. Most likely you are the one putting cash on their debit card, so they can grab lunch or go to a movie with friends. I'll stop here and give you credit! Teens and cash are a horrible idea—a teen on a cash diet is free to spend money however they see fit, free from moral, legal, or any sort of parent-aided prioritization and oversight. However, these sites are clever, and make it easier to hide purchases by obtaining business aliases for transaction records. So you might see an unusual purchase, but not fully vet it in the same way that you might if it read: FakeIDs.Org.

So how do they get the money to the online company if you don't see any charges? Well ... I hate to break it to you, but one of their friends' parents is marginalizing your parenting. Now mind you, this marginalization might be pure ignorance—for example parents who pay off their teen's credit card statement without really considering the transactions. This is very common with affluent and busy professionals. The next kind of parent is rather infuriating: it is the one who knows what is going on, doesn't care, thinks it's okay (see list at beginning of this section to jog your memory). And this is how it normally works. One teen serves as the point person, collecting payments, pictures, addresses etc. from "customers," uploads all the information onto the website, obtains the IDs and then upsells them back to the well-watched peer for profit.

Anecdotal example of why teens don't need a fake ID: When I was working as a school administrator I had the wonderful task of managing student parking. With limited parking, this was primarily for seniors. A senior boy came into the office to obtain his parking permit, which meant filling out his application including his driver's license number and address. Any guesses? This young man, 18 years old, rushed, filled out his application using his fake ID. I'd like to point out that in California, licenses face opposite directions based on the age threshold; if you're 21, your license is horizontal, and if you're not 21 yet, it's vertical. After he left the application, my assistant noticed that he had left his ID. He had filled out the entire application with his fake ID: same name, yes, but different address. Simple mistake, right? But this is an example of exactly why parents should not be giving or allowing young adults or old teenagers to have them. One who cannot notice that type of omission, lacks the basic decision-making qualities one needs to responsibly consume alcohol. Part of my duty in that role was to alert his parents. Unsurprised by my find, or his paperwork mistake, they had already found two other IDs in the past month in his room or wallet. So, his online purchase came with three.

Why it's a bad move to enable your teen's fake ID habit: Managing teenagers is all about managing expectations. Let's imagine behaviors are like an allowance: the more teenagers get in the form of freedoms, the more they spend, and the more they want and perceive to need in the future. So, for a high school student to have the blessing of a fake ID is only setting them up for further, more elevated, riskier, and age-inappropriate asks in the future. Have you ever tried putting the extra toothpaste that comes out back into the tube? How'd that work out for you? Giving permissive, misdemeanor or felony worthy permissions to your teenager is an extremely slippery slope, regardless of the qualifiers you place on your decision to allow it.

Legal Ramifications: There are undeniable legal consequences that impact those who choose to obtain and use a fake ID. Of course, this is hard to accept for those who feel invisible—like teenagers. For example, in California, Penal Code 470b makes it a crime to either display or possess a fake ID. Depending on the circumstances—how it's used, who provides goods or services based on it, etc.—there are various potential legal consequences. On the low end of the consequential scale, penalties if treated as a misdemeanor include a $1,000 fine and up to 1 year in County jail. If treated as a felony, the payoff is more significant with up to 3 years in jail and a $10,000 fine. Not to mention making a new friend in the form of a parole officer, the mark on their record, a cloud hanging over future college or graduate school admissions, and effective unemployability in many attractive and lucrative career fields.

Permissive Drinking: Fake IDs go hand-in-hand with the unfortunate miscalculation that many parents make when allowing their teenagers to openly and shamelessly consume alcohol. And I'm not talking about letting your son or daughter have a glass of wine with dinner at grandma's 80th birthday; I'm talking about binge drinking. Permissive drinking lives on the same slippery slope as enabling your teen with a fake ID. More times than not, teens don't get to a place overnight where they are regularly drinking in excess. Rather, they find themselves there based on the framework or roadmap that is often inadvertently provided for them by subtle permissive tactics.

Here are a few examples of permissive tactics:

✓ Allowing them to go to a party, but instructing them to have only a couple of drinks

✓ Allowing them to spend the night, anywhere, after age 12

✓ Allowing your teen to drink in your house because it's "safer"

✓ Allowing consumption based on neighborhood or peer group pressures

✓ Allowing it because it's easier (in the short term) than managing it

Alcohol permitted by good grades: There's an alarming sense of normalcy sitting firmly behind the parental practice of accepting, allowing, or turning a bling eye to teenage drinking so long as they keep their grades in order. Teenagers are aware of this trend and work hard academically to get the longer leash required to consume heavily, often, and dangerously.

How parents fall into this trap:

★ **By accident:** You had no idea they were partying; their good grades and clean discipline record rendered a long leash and you trust them. There is no indication that they might be up to no good and engaging in adult behaviors.

★ **Out of convenience:** Your kids are no good trapped in the house. You know that their friends drink sometimes, but you don't know what to do about it. It's okay for them to be around it, as it frees up your own time to relax, work out, be social, and spend time with your spouse.

★ **Path of least resistance:** You tried long and hard to stave off drinking and parties. But, inevitably, the teen reached a certain age and it became more work than it was worth to prevent it. You do your best to contain it, monitor it from afar, but all seems okay and they are simply a teenager doing the same things you did as a teenager.

★ **Focusing on the wrong success markers:** Grades and college are the priority. You cannot stop them from doing what they will do, so long as they fall in alignment with the academic standards set forth in your home. They are allowed (actively or passively) to engage in drinking because they've earned it with good grades and admission to a top tier college.

Dangers of allowing grade-based partying:

★ **The inevitable toll on long-term health:** Consuming alcohol regularly, and binge drinking occasionally, deprives teenagers of much needed sleep. It dehydrates them, affecting their athletics and intellectual capacities. Alcohol is known to serve as a depressant that may cause anxiety in teenagers and lead to isolative and erratic behavior.

★ **The eventual collapse of academic performance built of haphazard habits:** When students only work in short, sporadic increments to attain social privileges, they forgo building skills that endure over time. Study habits and a sound sense of academic integrity are forfeited in lieu of a quick fix to repair a low grade. As they progress through the academic channels of high school and then college, higher standards and more output expected from teachers and professors is hard to maintain without the proper habits. Eventually, your student will hit a ceiling, and no longer be able to wing it. And when it comes crashing down, it will crash hard, fast, and dramatically.

★ **The next-level substance use and abuse born of social partying:** What begins as recreational often leads to habitual. The buzz of a beer, stone of a joint, or fix of a vape shifts from a chosen action to a needed one when use increases. Having heard many first-hand accounts of addiction, the stories differ. Some recall being hooked from the very first instance of use, whereas others recall more of a crescendo, where frequency and dependency gained strength over time until its appeal was valued over everything else.

★ **Rewarding the wrong kind of success doesn't translate into expected results:** Earning a 4.0 GPA or admission to a university means little when the student lacks functionality and autonomy to thrive in that environment. Either the students have developed chemical dependency that stonewalls their ability to succeed at the next academic level, or they lack the basic, intrinsically driven tools to handle the rigor. So, while they were able to have their cake and eat it too in high school, it is often a recipe for disaster in college.

Parent Examples: The person who teenagers look to the most as an example is their parents. Mind you, they might not like you, be nice to you, or listen to you, but they're watching you. They look for permission to do what they want to do in what you are doing. And in this case, they watch your attitude, approach, use, and relationship with substances. Too many times, I've discussed with teenagers their use of substances only to find them validating their own actions based on their parents'. Yes, you are an adult, a professional, work hard, highly educated etc.; and I get it, you want to unwind and have an enjoyable time. That's fine, but please be aware of the responsibility ripple created in the family swimming pool. Watching your own consumption rate and habits is a terrific way to lead by example. Do what I say, not what I do, is an approach of diminishing returns. For a toddler who isn't allowed to eat anywhere but at the table, it may work, as you eat pizza on the couch watching the news. But, as your teens become acutely aware that you are drinking too much, too often, in all social settings—they assume they are receiving permission via osmosis.

Tips to strengthen your parent example:

★ Limit your consumption both in scope and scale (how much, how often).
  ☆ It's hard to parent effectively from a "do what I say, not as I do" point of view.

★ Choose nonalcoholic drinks when you go to a sporting event or concert with your teen.
  ☆ Training your teen to associate fun with alcohol is a dangerous game, but showing them that they can have a good time, as can you, sans the chardonnay is a winning combination.

★ Avoid "pre-partying" at tailgates prior to sporting events when in the presence of teens.
  ☆ Especially at collegiate or high school events—it's the same as above in that it sets a standard that alcohol is commiserate with fun; it's not.

★ Remain legally able to drive and pick them up from social gatherings.
　　☆ It's basically impossible to return in a conversation (at least with any kind of leverage) after your teen points out that the ONLY reason they took a ride sharing service home was that YOU were drunk.

★ Be open and willing to discuss your own shortcomings and mistakes; nothing enrages teens more than adults refusing to admit a mistake.
　　☆ Information is power. Don't give it all away, but be willing to relate to your teen's life or situation based on your own learning experiences.

Ride Sharing: As prefaced by the story at the beginning of this chapter, ride sharing has changed the game of teenage freedoms and drinking. I understand that it takes precision-like logistics to get all family members to the appropriate place, at the appropriate time. Ride sharing apps are wonderful for trips to the airport, when a car breaks down, and to navigate through times when kids are double booked and only one parent, or no parents, can get them to their required destination. I am not admonishing ride sharing in terms of its viability within many benign circumstances. Ride sharing, however, has done an excellent job of subtly eroding the long tradition of children and younger teens getting to and from social gatherings by parents, and older teens driving themselves home (responsibly and sober). Let's review the pros and cons of ride sharing.

Ride sharing upsides:

✓ Family logistics and problem solving

✓ Real-time geo-fencing that provides location, pick up/drop off points, time, ETA, cost etc.

✓ Less hands-on parenting in terms of driving and managing your adult schedule around your teen's

✓ Less conflict regarding attending social events based on logistical limitations

Ride sharing downsides:

✓ Teen's become unavoidably mobile, which is often too tempting.

✓ Curfews get pushed, tested and omitted with more frequency.

✓ Parents themselves become more social, less accountable, potentially being unable to attend to a teen in need based on their own consumption or unavailability.

✓ The teen is unarguably more vulnerable than if they were being transported by their parent or the parent of a friend. It doesn't take many searches to return a batch of results where intoxicated female riders were sexually assaulted by their driver. I know the odds are low; but still, can you imagine the regret of that incident if attached to your choice as the parent to enable or even openly fund that ride in lieu of your own pick up or drop off?

Tips regarding ride sharing:

★ Use it as needed, but avoid night time transport. I have clients who apologize profusely to me when sending their student to my office via a ride-sharing service. There's no judgement there, if it's valid and logistically needed. A 3:00 pm ride to an appointment is very different than an 11:30 pm pick up to a random house party as you're out of town or fast asleep after a few too many martinis after work.

★ Monitor your teen's bank statements to look for such rides. I worked with a student once who, as an eighth grader, had an account and actively used it for about eight months prior to his parents finding out. His method was impressively strategic: he would frontload it and back it up with purchases of comparable price so that it would seemingly blend in. And it worked! In fact, the only reason he was caught was that he fell victim to being a young man void of fully developed decision-making skills. One day, after school, while attempting to impress some would-be friends, he ordered the souped-up SUV, took everyone to the mall, racked up a big charge, and spoiled his own free-range enterprise.

★ If you do decide you are willing to let your teen utilize ride-sharing services, be certain to monitor it closely. The geofencing features on most apps allow you to see location in real time, as well as any financial costs associated with rides. Here's a hint: if they have a $150 service fee ... someone threw up.

Binge drinking: There's a saying in the world of addiction that goes like this: you have the first drink, and the second drink has you. That is very true with adults who are suffering from addiction, but also, it's very true for teenagers with access to alcohol. Go big or go home. A common tactic that I find parents employing is allowing their child to have alcohol, but only to a certain extent. Parents might let their child go to a party where booze is served, and leave with the parting instructions that the teen is to have only X amount of X. *You can go, but only have three beers, okay.* Other times the qualifier is that they may drink, but not a specific kind of alcohol. *You can have a good time, but no hard alcohol.* But as the saying goes, they have the first drink, and the second drink has them. This saying can mean a lot of things based on the variables a teen will encounter when partying. They could have the first drink, and that drink could have something in it, like a drug, or a pill, or be mixed with god-knows-what.

Tips to combat binge drinking

★ **Drop off/pick up:** For whatever reason, teens seem to think that if they get a ride home with someone else they will have time to sober up. Lol. The absence of logic in this assertion is funny, but sadly adopted by many. The difference between teens who won't get hammered and those who will? Parents. The teens who have a parent arriving to pick them up are less likely to have anything to drink, let alone too much to drink.

★ **Ditch sleepovers:** Honestly, if you're still allowing your teenage to sleep at a friend's house, shame on you. I say that with love. But sleepovers are a teenager's dream. First, sleepovers tend to occur at the house with the path of least resistance: the friend with parents out of town, their own wing of the house, parents who are generally "cool," or those who won't tell other parents when their child is barfing in their guest bathroom at midnight. Second, sleepovers rarely occur where they were intended to. I'm telling you, you think you're allowing your daughter to sleep at one of her good friend's houses, but turns out, her parents think the same thing, too. In reality, they are really staying at friend number three's house. You know, the one with the "cool" parents. Good luck with that.

★ **Breathalyze:** Not always. Just often enough to keep 'em guessing. Teens prey on the predictability of their parents. Combat this with being just unpredictable enough to prevent bad choices and too many sips on the 'ol wine cooler.

Pharma-Russian roulette: Another alarming trend in the quest for a good high is the abuse of prescription medication. You name the prescription, and a teen your teen knows is actively hypothesizing and testing that high-seeking hypothesis, as to whether it will produce a worthy buzz. For the sake of a more specific focus on this subtopic, let's look at the drugs associated with mood disorders and attention deficit disorders. These are the go-to, and most accessible for teens. The prescriptions, though well intended and properly prescribed to the teenage patients, often find their ways into the hands and bloodstreams of those for which the script was not intended, or for the patient, but mixed with other substances, like alcohol, that can result in a fatal overdose.

Medications intended to treat attention deficit, "uppers," and medications intended to treat anxiety, "downers," are fan favorites on the high school scene. It's very common for teens to hoard and sell their pills to peers, either because they don't like the way it makes them feel, or for cash flow, or both. Again, I'm not a clinician, and make no claims regarding medication, but I've seen it too many times for it not to be true: teens share their medications if they can. This is where you, the parent, can help end this cycle.

Tips for dealing with pharma

★ **Distribute the medication:** I know this may feel too *Cuckoo's Nest* but hear me out. If you take the time to simply give your teen their one pill, watch them drink it down, and do it with a relaxed normalcy wrapped into the rest of your morning routine, they will be less likely to not take the medicine, let alone hoard it for distribution later. Remember, teens are simply capitalizing where there is opportunity. I know plenty of nice, well-intended students who began stashing their pills after realizing no one had any idea as to whether they took it or not.

★ **Talk to your child about their medication:** Many teens that I know who have ended up distributing pills for cash did so because they didn't want to be taking the medicine in the first place. Maintaining an open channel of communication with your child about the medicine is a key ingredient to preventing such issues. Of course, you want to be sure to include your medical team in any changes to their medications, but the process begins at home. If your teen feels that there is zero chance you will allow them not to take the medicine, then they will turn to other, more sketchy options.

★ **Drug test:** Many students who aren't drinking alcohol, smoking weed, or even vaping, are in fact, abusing prescription medications. Around final exams, there is a significant spike in teens seeking "uppers" to help them bend time and stay up all night cramming. Likewise, there are many who are so stressed out about their grades, the impact on college admissions, whether they're going to get grounded, that they buy some "downers" to stave off their anxious moments. I advise having your pediatrician periodically drug test even the most seemingly innocent teens in order to look for substances that may start with desperation and end up with full-fledged addiction or a serious medical complication.

Evolution and legalization of marijuana: Marijuana sure has come a long way since I was in high school. Most obviously, its legalization and acceptance into the medicinal realm has effectively complicated the narrative and made it more difficult to limit access. I make no claims as to the legalization or medicinal debate, but I do feel, like with alcohol, that the earlier one begins to consume, the more potential that trouble and addiction looms. As is well documented with many items that are legal, they are not always appropriate or healthy for individuals.

Mainstream media: One aspect to marijuana that has not changed, yet has become more common, is the glamorization of its use. Many well-known, much-streamed artists reference, post pictures on social media, and openly endorse marijuana. This can be challenging for teens to process, and parents to properly combat, as the same people who they emulate and strive to become are championing, or at least validating, the use of the drug. In addition to the fight to stave off use within the context of your own parenting and family philosophy, you are also battling the ever-present struggle by the teen to fit in and maintain their street-cred.

Not your generation's weed: Just like the car you drive, the phone you use, the TV you watch, and light bulbs you put into your lamp—weed has evolved in a scientific sense. Basically, it's stronger than ever. While some may be quick to dismiss the use of marijuana by comparing it to the effects it had on them at a similar age, this is an outdated reference point. What's more, copycats emulate the marijuana experience via creating a liquid form of the drug. One example is the street name Dabs, which is an equivalent in the wax format. I've seen the devastating reaction that kids have had to the drug. I know kids who have ingested the drug and found themselves overdosing, and in the ICU within hours. Unlike alcohol, which has clearly marked alcohol by volume percentages to at least give some sense of its strength, the marijuana market, especially in the way that teens obtain it, is largely a choose your own adventure scenario. If there is one benefit to the medicinal angle of the marijuana market, it's that it provides for transparency of product. What type it is, the anticipated effects, strength and so on. However, just like all drugs intended for medical purposes, they are only intended for those prescribed.

Drug testing: Drug testing is a straightforward way (not to sound too obvious) to know what substances your teen is using. A variety of methods exist for testing including at-home kits, or trips to the pediatrician or Urgent Care. Whatever the case, before you initiate a test, have a plan in place in terms of what steps you will take upon learning the results.

Here are some common drug testing mistakes made by parents:

- Warning or prefacing their child regarding drug test
  - Parent: "We're going to drug test you every Monday."
  - Teen thinks to self: "Perfect, I'll just smoke weed through Thursday, and buy a urine cleansing kit online to wash it away."
- Threatening, but never facilitating the drug test
  - Parent: "I'm going to drug test you when you get back from spring break in Cabo."
  - Teen (a week later): "My parents always says they'll drug test me, but never do ... let's rip!"
- Avoiding a doctor's office drug test for fear of others "knowing"
  - It's called HIPAA; there are strict laws in place for privacy. Moreover, part of getting the best medical attention is

including your pediatrician in the process. Perhaps they will connect a dot that your untrained eyes cannot see.

● Issuing a drug test with no plan in place

  ○ Parent: "You've tested positive for marijuana and Xanax!"

  ○ Parent, again: "One more failed drug test and we're going to send you away."

*As stated in the three prior failed drug tests

Drug testing suggestions

★ **Understand what you are looking for.**

  ☆ Over the counter drug testing kits come with varying degrees of sophistication. Often referred to as "panels," tests will screen for certain substances, but not all. For example, suspicious parents might be intent on looking for marijuana, therefore test for marijuana, but miss less notable or less obvious prescription drugs. I've known clients to pass standard drug tests, only to fail ones via a doctor's office or treatment facility.

★ **Politely ambush your teenager.**

  ☆ If I wasn't clear earlier, warning your teenager about drug tests allows them to build the infrastructure to either pass them strategically: either by careful timeline of use, or by obtaining others' urine, or by using drugs that you aren't testing for.

  ☆ If you've arrived at the point of drug testing, privacy has gone out the window. That said, when you are testing at home, you need to monitor the test. Yes, watch them pee. Door open. Carefully. If you want the truth, it needs to be transparent. Trust is not the real issue here; if you're testing, there's already a trust issue, and the test is a method for your teenager to earn back that trust.

★ **Break the cycle of secrecy and go to the doctor.**

  ☆ The doctor is the doctor. They are trained medical professionals and can access tests far more effective than what you can use at home. Plus, they know how to read them, monitor the process, and have a network of resources and options for parents upon a positive result. Part of breaking the cycle of use and dishonesty is rooted in disrupting routine. Going to the doctor sends a clear message that you are in charge, they are a child, and others will know if they are using. I get it that you don't want your neighbors or Aunt Kathy to know, but keeping this issue to yourself is a deeply risky move unless you are trained in navigating adolescent substance use.

★ **Use the cancer analogy.**

☆ This is not intended to diminish those suffering from cancer, but to draw a parallel from one disease to another. If your child was manifesting symptoms of cancer, you would have them tested by a doctor. You wouldn't buy an at-home cancer test and then wishy-wash your way around the results. *Maybe it's just a cancer phase.* You wouldn't. So why embrace that thinking with drug addiction or alcoholism? Addiction is a disease and needs to be treated accordingly; trying to qualify it or make social or financial excuses to explain why you can't afford to tell anyone, or afford the cost to address the issue, is a losing approach, and a disservice to the very child you brought into this world.

★ **Vet your resources and have a plan in place.**

☆ What, exactly, are you going to do if your child tests positive for drugs? Think about it.

Does your insurance cover:
- Therapy (psychologist, or psychiatrist)
    Maybe begin here to dig for the "root"
    of their use
- Outpatient treatment
    Typically, either half-day or full-day programs
- In-patient, residential treatment
    Typically, a minimum of 30 days followed by ongoing outpatient and mental health services and appointments

Your teenager and marijuana: Let's use marijuana as our baseline for this process. For the learning process in this portion of the book to work, it's important to have an open mind. I know, I know ... it's not relevant to you or your teen. And I'm sure you're right, or at least I hope you are. The *not my kid* philosophy is common but dangerous, as it can often prevent parents from planning a response to negative behaviors. It's the same kind of stock-photo invincibility that teenagers themselves employ to assure others (and themselves) that their reckless choices are simply normal teenage shenanigans that will not lead to further negative actions and should not lead to parent intervention or interference.

Okay, so weed. Your teen wants to smoke a bowl, or pipe, or vape, or eat a brownie. They want to get stoned AF [as f*ck]. So, there you are. As a parental team you have deduced that the symptoms you've observed equate to probable cause that your teen is using drugs. So, like any alarmed parent you race to the pediatrician or pharmacy to obtain a drug testing kit. This is where many parents get stuck: they race out and buy, hurry up and give, and then quickly have a positive drug test result in their hands. But then what? In a linear sense, the now what would seemingly fit nicely at the end of this pattern, right? Yes, but not so. Really, the now what phase needs to be in place prior to the purchase of the test.

Give them this kind of permission: Teenagers love the permission you give them not to use drugs. That permission needs to be very clear. This is a fitting example of how teenagers cannot see grey. They only see black and white. What is allowed. What is not allowed. What will happen when they cross the line. One of the first mistakes that parents make is that they over promise and under deliver. I'm pretty sure this is the opposite of the common sales phrase of *under promise and over deliver*. It's easy to fall into this trap. Yelling threats that you will never, ever, ever, follow through on. *I'm going to send you to wilderness camp! See if you can survive out there with the wolves.* Okay. This isn't to knock wilderness as an intervention. I'm not trained on interventions like this, but from what I've been told, there is certainly a time, place, circumstance or action that can be successfully addressed when teens are removed from their current environment and work with the appropriate professionals. And sometimes that's in the woods. But the logistics, and costs, and emotions that must be fully aligned and available in order to actuate that ideation into a concrete plan of action are astronomical. So the more you make grand claims like sending your teenagers to places like wilderness camp without a) actually needing that big of an intervention; or b) ever following through, the more idle your threats become. Instead of being the parents who send your teen to the wilderness to be near wolves, you will be the parents who keep them in the suburbs and cry wolf.

But the plausibility of follow-through is a crucial hurdle that many parents cannot get over. Teens love to call the bluff of adults; it's what I enjoyed doing most myself as a teen. So, when they are bong-in-hand on the 4th of July, their internal filter is flipping through their childhood accountability rolodex looking for indicators of your level of follow-through. *Well, I never actually make curfew, and nothing happens,* or *My older brother came home super hammered and boked* [threw up] *all over the bathroom yet still went out the next weekend.* These examples are more direct offenses and slights to your parenting. But many times, teens' actions are much more slight and subtle (with each of them not really equating to much on their own). However, the accountability rolodex doesn't care; it simply analyzes actions and (lack of) consequences to quickly determine whether the bong hits the lips. Teens look for follow-through, in all forms.

But you can't go back in time to reimplement or reassert yourself as a parent into situations that are long gone. What you can do, however, is reestablish or reengage into the active parenting process.

So, weed. A few questions to use in this quest for greater planning:

○ What is your own experience with marijuana?

○ For example, are you afraid of condemning the joint you once held in your own hand?

○ How did drug use negatively impact your own life or the lives of loved ones?

○ How has age and time changed your perspective of drug use?

○ What fears do you have regarding your children and marijuana use?

○ Perhaps there are certain people, or kinds of people you fear they'll become, or they are becoming.

By asking yourself questions like these, you will begin to better understand your philosophy behind marijuana. In facing your philosophy and asserting it into your parenting plan, you are more likely to follow through with your planned course of action; but also, be able to articulate your rationale to your teen.

Marijuana and nicotine diagnostic

Directions: Using the list below, identify all that apply to you or your teenager.

☐ I allow its use.

☐ allow its use in our home.

☐ I allow other teens to use marijuana or nicotine at home.

☐ I get permission from parents before allowing marijuana or nicotine use.

☐ I don't allow marijuana or nicotine use.

☐ I have clear consequences if it's used.

☐ I have never had an incident with my teen and marijuana or nicotine.

☐ I know they smoke but haven't addressed the issue.

☐ My teen does not use marijuana or nicotine.

☐ My teen uses ridesharing apps.

☐ I allow my teen's friends to stay over if they've been smoking.

☐ I talk to my teen about the dangers of marijuana and nicotine.

☐ I have no idea if my teen smokes.

☐ I don't want to know if my teen smokes.

☐ I assume they smoke, because I did when I was their age.

☐ I know which families allow teens to smoke at their homes.

Unpacking the diagnostic: Take a minute to review your answers—what boxes you checked. I find the act of writing things down, in plain view, free from judgement is the best way to understand the current state of marijuana use within your family structure. What speaks to you? Is there anything you intentionally skipped? Did you experience any twinges of guilt or shame or embarrassment with this list? Would you show it to your neighbor?

Personal Reflection

Directions: Based on the previous exercise, rate yourself on the following sliding scales.

My overall awareness of my teen's marijuana use is:

○ High

○ Elevated

○ Neutral

○ Low

○ Nonexistent

My overall contribution to their marijuana use is:

- ○ High
- ○ Elevated
- ○ Neutral
- ○ Low
- ○ Nonexistent

My overall concern regarding marijuana use is:

- ○ High
- ○ Elevated
- ○ Neutral
- ○ Low
- ○ Nonexistent

Knowing where you stand: As stated before, it is important that both you and your teen know your philosophy regarding marijuana and the values that support that philosophy. Teens need consistency; no one wins when one weekend they are permitted to use marijuana, the next they are not; or in one instance there is a consequence from its use, but in another there is not.

Task: In the chart below, take a few minutes to evaluate your stance, position, rules and consequences regarding your teen and marijuana use. This is a personal, family decision. This section is not intended to tell you what to do. Rather it is meant to heighten your awareness regarding your philosophy and the values behind it. It is vital to be clear about the rules, expectations, and consequences with your teen.

My philosophy:	My values:

My rules:	The consequences:

Vaping: When I'm asked to pinpoint the one, most significant drug of choice right now, I would tell you it's nicotine.

You right now: my kid doesn't smoke! Me to you right now: lol.

Again, much like our conversation about marijuana, nicotine is experiencing its own renaissance now. It's true, you won't find teens smoking cigarettes in the bathrooms, or while shooting pool, or behind the drive-in theatre like you did as a teen. No, what they're up to is much more rampant and significantly easier to hide from parent or school official eyes and intuition. Teens today are all about using nicotine in its liquid form, free from the tar or "smoke" of cigarettes. Sure, hardcore teens still rock their good old-fashioned smokes, but for the most part, they've gone all in with vaping.

Why they vape: In short, vaping is done for street cred. Think about it, how do you socially assimilate, without getting drunk or high? You vape. Vaping offers the best of both worlds, a short, subtle high or buzz, without the worry of "getting rolled" by parents for being intoxicated or wreaking of substances the next day. Teenagers often refer to the effect of vaping as a "dome"—a short, 30-second euphoric high produced by the high concentration of nicotine. Social integration and a "dome" are the initial reasons they vape, but the next is the gnarly one: they're addicted. Addicted. Let that sink in. It's a polarizing word, and one that both the teen vaping constantly and their parents who eventually catch them tend to embrace. In my work, I have discovered the world of vaping knows no stereotype or social architype. I can tell you, like they'll tell you, they literally all vape.

Ease of use: Vaping is certainly a user friendly teenage habit. They'll small, easy to hide, hard to catch, often odorless, and traded on the teenage black market that makes it the easiest substance to get. I recall when vapor nicotine hit the market, and they were the size of a 1993 cell phone. One of those original vapes was not high-school friendly. But now, they are the size of a pen ... a pen. What's more? They come in trendy, fruity flavors to satisfy even the pickiest teen vaper. I regularly hear stories from high school students about peers vaping in class, while the teacher is teaching, and the teacher has no clue. The kids know, and it bothers many of them, but more than not, there is a resounding code of silence. For one, no teen wants to be pegged as a nark; but also, there is a primal teenage amusement that the teacher cannot tell that someone is VAPING in their classroom WHILE they are teaching. I can't.

Side effects: I am not a medical professional and I'm not going to list the health effects. But if you ask a teen, there is a commonly accepted mindset that vaping is not smoking, and therefore not bad for you. This reminds me of my own father's stories about cigarette companies sending reps onto his high school campus to distribute samples. No one, according to him, viewed it as bad for your health. Today, many kids won't do it because they *think it's gross* but there is not a straight line between use of nicotine in its vape form and buzz words like cancer, as it exists with traditional cigarette consumption. My fear is that vaping is like the wild west right now, and in about twenty years from now medical professionals will have enough data points and case studies to condemn its use much like the way it went down with big tobacco. And while ambiguity might exist regarding health, make no mistake about it, vaping is both extremely expensive and addictive.

Your teen's response to the opportunity to use or abuse substances depends largely on the foundation you've installed at home.

Let's analyze the factors that tip the scales (in one direction or the other) when they are confronted with the opportunity to *party*. And it's not the innocent birthday party from the days of long ago. Rather, for the sake of this analysis, let's assume that your teenager is attending a party where the booze is flowing like water, compliments of an older sibling's new fake ID. Of course, why your teen is at the party in the first place is the subplot, but we will touch on that later in the book; for now, let's just use the dynamics of the party. Your teen. Alcohol. Opportunity.

Use this visual to metaphorically process your teenager's response to temptation. Within your teen's body, your teen represents the backbone, their opportunity to drink alcohol represents gravity, and you, the parents, are the muscle. We know that without muscle, the body cannot stand up straight and with age, gravity takes a toll on the body. A simple fact exists that teenagers are big children, but still children. And children do not have the internal fortitude or decision-making skeletal system that we, as adults, have. Your teenager's response to the gravity of the temptation will be inherently attached to your parental muscle. Not the *I'm going to kill you if you ever drink* (though that is one strategy), but in general, how well you have laid the groundwork for all things alcohol: rules, consequences, effects, health, peer pressure, legal ramifications ... all of it.

The arrival: Upon arriving to said party, it becomes quickly apparent that kids are drinking. Now these are not just any kids either; no, these kids are your child's friends. These kids are your child's classmates, teammates, camp roommates, neighbors ... the contacts in their phone. Their Instagram followers. Ultimately, the decision will be, and is very much about more than just alcohol and whether or not to consume it. It's about their backbone, the weight of social gravity, and you, the muscle.

The temptation: The party, as they say, is lit. When it's time to (potentially) drink booze, and that seems to be the expected or socially implied behavior within their peer-friend-group-reality, your teen quickly evaluates the cost-benefit analysis of said partying through the filter of your family paradigm to reach a conclusion. To party or not to party: that is the question. Now without a doubt on the course of their road to adulthood, your teen will face countless decisions and ultimately determine that they're gonna do it anyhow. There will, without fail, be times when your teenager, regardless of what that family paradigm filter tells or cautions, proceed with the poorer of available choices. However, in many cases, and more typically with younger teenagers, that family paradigm filter will prevent or delay their early substance use. And any delay of substance use is a win. A one-day delay is a win. A one-year delay, a bigger win. And so forth. Which, if you spend any time on Google, researching substance abuse, you will quickly learn that the earlier one begins partying, the more prone they are to develop a problem with substances. In this scenario, and many similar scenarios, the teen weighs the cost/benefit between the amount of the street cred the proposed action or behavior will provide them with their peers, and the weight of the consequences or potential consequences at home.

The decision: Their moral filtration process goes something like this: how many likes will this snap of me and my cru with Jello shots get me vs. how many weeks of isolation and no phone will my parent issue. Computing. Aaannnd. Decision. *Shots! Shots! Shots!* **or** *I can't; I have to get up really early tomorrow and play volleyball.*

Create rules that are black and white: Teens see in black and white. They know in a nano-second, or at least they decide in one, the risk versus reward or cost-benefit analysis of whatever social pressure they're facing. They know how soft, or tough, or consistent, or inconsistent their parents are. They know which parent to target. Which parent to attack. Which parent to guilt. Which parent to ignore. Which parent to fear. And so on. So if you have not, with explicit clarity and effective simplicity and protracted consistency, provided your teenager with the relevant information to make that decision, you will end up asking them about the Jello shots (right after you clean up the barf in the guest bathroom). Let me repeat the three key words in the engaged parenting model: simplicity, clarity, and consistency.

Make your rules simple: I was recently told that the average adult has the attention span of seven seconds. I literally cannot remember who told me that. But I'm using it because it proves the point that they were most likely right. If I'm a teenager who lovingly refers to my parents by their first names out of bitter spite, my attention span is even shorter than seven seconds; and it's even shorter when it involves things likes rules and personal accountability. Rules and family guidelines should be concise. They should be easy to remember and hard to manipulate. The teenage brain is less than stellar in the fully-developed or I-can-plan-anything-well categories, so the least we can do is not exacerbate these annoyances any further. A common landmine of over-complication is curfew. *It's 10:00pm on Friday, unless it's a special occasion, then it's 11:00pm; if you have club volleyball in the morning then it's 9:00pm sharp, unless your practice is at 10:00am, then you can stay out until 9:30pm.* I appreciate your flexibility. I really do. But the average teenager cannot even remember to fully charge their phone or pack all necessary items in their backpack, let alone keep this schedule in their brain. The more variances, the more conflict. If you want conflict, have lots of variances. If you seek less conflict, have less variances. Perhaps your curfew goes something like this: *tell me what you want to do, where, with whom, how I can contact their parents, and why this is a responsible choice ... and I'll tell you if you can go and when to be home.* This strategy works well. Questions like these reduce requests. And when your teenagers give you the answers to said questions, you should have nearly, if not all, the necessary information to make your curfew decision.

Tips for simplicity.

★ Make a list of all of the rules you currently have in play within the management of your teen.

★ Look for overlap and try to consolidate the rules into fewer rules where possible. For example, if there are layers to curfew, try to reduce those layers and come up with one time. Maybe two. But less is more.

★ Avoid overcomplicating your rules. More complicated sets of rules lead to more grey area, which in turn leads to ambiguity, which certainly results in confusion and conflict. For example, they can either use ride sharing apps or not. Not sometimes yes, and sometimes no.

Make your rules clear and easy to understand by eliminating variables from the conversation: Nothing like ambiguity to really shake things up in a tense, teenage-dwelling household. One seemingly obvious, yet gravely underutilized strategy is to keep your rules to a minimum. Teenagers can only see in black and white. Things either are, or they are not. Teens don't do very well with grey. Grey areas, in-betweens, exceptions, one-time-onlys, often simply lead to chaos and conflict. You'll get caught in the *last time you let me* trap and that's no fun. Boundaries need to be clearly marked. They need rules, guidelines, criteria, etc., to be explicit. Easy to read. Easy to understand. Straightforward. But we just can't help ourselves sometimes as parents and adults; we love to complicate things. Just look at the DMV. Or trying to split a bill at a group dinner. It's way harder than it needs to be sometimes. The same is true with rules. If you need a flow chart to understand the rules in your household, it's time to start over.

In the spirit of clarity, utilizing an umbrella approach to managing teens works well for many families. There should be an overarching umbrella of base-core-value rules in place. Once established and known, they can guide your decision-making process. Some examples of base-core-value rules are: *be respect-*

ful, be honest, be responsible, and *be safe.* Notice they are not saying what *not* to do. Kind of like at the pool; lifeguards often say *walk please* instead of screaming *no running!* So once your four core rules are in place, then pick a few (seriously, just a few) practical rules, like that of a curfew, to embrace. Other practical rules typically address substances (alcohol, drugs, vape, nicotine), grades, social media, cell phone, Internet, and general antics. The more you have, the more you have to deal with establishing clarity. Too many rules and they are less meaningful, and eventually less likely to be enforced.

Tips for clarity.

★ Keep your rules in check; the more rules you employ the less meaningful those rules become.

★ Define an umbrella of base-core values to drive your rule-making process.

★ Remind your teens of these core values before they leave and when they return.

★ For example, on the way out the door instead of nagging with *you better be home by ten!* you can instead shift the mantra to something more positive such as *please remember to be respectful and safe tonight; have fun, we'll see you at ten!* Same message; very different delivery.

Be consistent: I grew up in the middle of nowhere, in teenager terms. To get anywhere involving a debit card or a stop light required a 30-minute-plus drive. That meant lots of speeding. That said, there was a big stretch of highway which we called *the reservoir* because you guessed it, it went by a reservoir. So, next to said water and about half way between point nowhere and point somewhere was the perfect place to really put the petal to the metal. It was the perfect stretch of road to go ham, save for one minor detail: the highway patrolman who was seemingly *always* there. *Does he sleep? Does he eat?* These were just some of the more PG questions we would ask ourselves as we moseyed on by at a meek 55mph. Now, this was arguably the most dangerous stretch of road, and one that could have resulted in accidents, or at the very least lots and lots of speeding tickets, for teen drivers. Not to say that some didn't get tickets, because they did, but most of the management strategy for this sketchy stretch of highway was built on one basic strategy: consistency. The man, or *The Man* as we referred to him, was there almost daily. There were no glaring inconsistencies in his proximity to the road. You wouldn't be able to say *he's never there on Monday; or he's only there in the morning.* No, he was there, consistently. So we teenage drivers obeyed the speed limit with mirrored consistency. We knew the rules, knew they were going to be enforced, witnessed them being enforced, and thus (mostly), obeyed them. All with little effort by *The Man*. He was good at his job.

Rules only work for parents when the parents use them consistently. If the child has to run through a reasoning sequence in their teenage brain in order to determine if you are actually going to follow through this time (as you have not in the past) then you have already lost this round. Consistency is a very underutilized wrench in the parenting toolbox. If you attach reasonable accountability measures (consequences) to the various rules you have in place (hopefully not too many rules!) and apply them consistently over time, your efforts will begin to pay off. The best wingman to consistency is stoicism. Being able to issue consequences with no tangible anger, sadness, or aggression is important to your success. While we all love to scream, cry, yell, or throw things across the living room, such actions pay little return in the context of issuing a consequence to a teenager. Remember: teenagers see in black and white. They don't have the capacity or the patience for too many variables.

Tips for consistency.

★ Pre-plan various interventions or consequences for typical or anticipated behaviors.

★ Always prepare for a bit worse than you can wrap your head around, just in case. There is nothing worse than being unprepared as a parent.

★ Treat your responses with less emotion than your mind, body, heart, and soul are demanding you do.

☆ The ability to posture calmly and void of over-the-top emotion will help you keep an advantageous position within the parent-teen dynamic. I get it, it is easy to let emotions seep to the surface and throw a riot straight out of your mouth and into the living room air. This is nothing short of a trap.

☆ You cannot unsay or un-throw what you say or throw; once those words hit the air, or vase hits the floor, the moment shifts from what your teen has done or said to what you have done or said.

☆ In short, if you are not careful, the moment will quickly become about you, when it should not be.

Simple, clear and consistent rules pay off: Teenagers face these split-second decisions hundreds of times during any given day. Do I drink? Do I cheat on this economics assignment? Do I bully this girl? Do I stay out just ten more minutes past curfew? Do I get to class on time? Do I forge this note and leave for lunch early? Do I wear these shorts even though they are potentially a dress code offense? Do I let him touch me, even though I'm not ready? Do I look at this website? Do I share my attention deficit disorder medication with my neighbor, so he can crush his English essay? Do I share the answers to my homework on this group chat? Do I take this bracelet without paying? Do I shoulder tap this dude at Circle K and ask him to buy me some vape? Do I use this ride-sharing app when I'm under strict orders not to? Do I? It's. Exhausting. And as if adding insult to injury, is the fact that teens really can't win ... when the answer to any of these examples is *no*, teens risk the exposure to the reverse cost/benefit analysis: the fallout from their peers; and when the answer to any of these questions is *yes*, they risk being grounded, arrested, detained, expelled, and so on.

I know, I know. Earlier I said we shouldn't feel sorry for teenagers and use that guilt to enable them. I'm not. I simply want to make it clear just how effed up being a teenager is in this current moment. And why it's even more important than ever to provide them with permission to detach, disengage, slow down, and take a breath. The gift of structure is one that can change a teenager's life.

For many teenagers, remaining largely conventional and normal requires a bit of selling-out. Unfortunately, for teens to attain and maintain this peer conventionality, the teenagers must say yes to many of the questions listed above. And that sucks. Thus, they sell out their own moral compass to keep up with their peers. The irony here is that it's a circular cluster *you know what*, that if they all just stopped, and took pause, they would or could realize that none of them really want to be hammered at 4:00pm on a Saturday afternoon. This sale of one's own personal choice seems to be a necessary evil. And that's where adults and parents are so vital. Adults have the remote, and can press pause. But so many of them don't know where the remote is. Or how to use it. Or it's out of batteries. Are we good?

Teenagers who make the sale (of their moral and ethical compass) are more widely accepted, and viewed as mainstream. Again, it's vital to acknowledge that for teenagers, and their overly stimulated and under-developed brains, it's not a conscious decision. They aren't actively choosing to be anything, really. Those who won't make the sale (especially at the teenage level) run the risk of becoming ostracized, especially if they refuse the sale and finger wag at those around them. The nuance in this quest for authenticity, is to attain it, while allowing others around them to maintain whatever state they choose to obtain.

Here are some tips for talking to your teenager about substances.

Use information as power: The approach many parents attempt is a no-excuses, no-discussion, no-means-no, because-I-said-so approach. This works well with some kids, and for others, it's not enough. Teenagers like to feel validated; they are school-going sponges who are expected to do things like provide supporting details and facts to prove their claims in essays and biology labs. That said, it's important to provide them with relevant information as to why they would be better off sipping on a coke and not beer. I don't suggest full-force fear mongering with random facts from the Internet. But smaller, more intimate, relevant pieces of information can go a long way in your cause. Personal anecdotes about your own mistakes are effective. Not five miles in the snow both ways vibes, but honest, vulnerable, and formative experiences. Your mistakes. Your lessons. Passed on. Family members' experiences with addiction, or mistakes involving substances are also valuable tools. Basically, it's key to wrap the rules in stories that make the rules understandable; they won't like the rules, but if they have more ground from which to understand them, you're better off than before.

Pick your examples carefully: When I was about twelve years old my dad took my older brother and me on an unannounced ride one morning. He said little and answered no questions about our journey as we made our way to a stretch of road with a silver pickup truck pulled off to the side. As we approached, he slowed to a crawl, and signaled us to look out the window. Dents and body damage soon led our eyes to broken windows, smeared with blood, and hair affixed to the cracks of glass. "Sean," he said, "was drinking and driving." Sean was a family friend, older, cool as could be, who he knew we looked up to. Sean was a relevant example, and one that I can say with certainty quelled any desire I ever had to drive buzzed. Where as one parent might list off the penal code or fines that accompany a DUI, my dad had an example that said much more, while saying almost nothing at all.

Get off the hamster wheel: Not to confuse you (I know only two bullets earlier I said that a hardline no-means-no approach might not work), but the hard line is still a good option for many parents. "No" is a complete sentence. Once you have laid the ground work that explains why your rules exist, with the stories, facts, moral attachments that you have outlined over time, there is really no reason to keep going around and around about your rules. Teenagers love to renegotiate the deal. And you let them into that process by opening the conversation (debate, really) about the rules. To be succinct, if every Saturday rolls around and inevitably your teen is looking for wiggle room to get boozy or whatever, a short, firm, friendly "no" is all you need. Of course, it's always fun to add just one new factoid or anecdote to the preface of that response to keep your rationale fluid and up-to-date. Teen: "Can I go out with the boys for a few beers?" Parent: "You know your cousin Justin just got kicked out of college for too many alcohol-related infractions ... oh, and, no."

Here are warning signs of substance abuse according to the National Council on Alcoholism and Drug Dependence

Physical and health signs of drug abuse

- Eyes that are bloodshot or pupils that are smaller or larger than normal.
- Frequent nosebleeds could be related to snorted drugs (meth or cocaine).
- Changes in appetite or sleep patterns. Sudden weight loss or weight gain.
- Seizures without a history of epilepsy.
- Deterioration in personal grooming or physical appearance.
- Impaired coordination, injuries/accidents/bruises that they won't or can't tell you about—they don't know how they got hurt.
- Unusual smells on breath, body, or clothing.
- Shakes, tremors, incoherent or slurred speech, impaired or unstable coordination.

Behavioral signs of alcohol or drug abuse

- Skipping class, declining grades, getting in trouble at school.
- Drop in attendance and performance at work—loss of interest in extracurricular activities, hobbies, sports or exercise—decreased motivation.
- Complaints from co-workers, supervisors, teachers or classmates.
- Missing money, valuables, prescription or prescription drugs, borrowing and stealing money.
- Acting isolated, silent, withdrawn, engaging in secretive or suspicious behaviors.
- Clashes with family values and beliefs.
- Preoccupation with alcohol and drug-related lifestyle in music, clothing and posters.
- Demanding more privacy, locking doors and avoiding eye contact.
- Sudden change in relationships, friends, favorite hangouts, and hobbies.
- Frequently getting into trouble (arguments, fights, accidents, illegal activities).
- Using incense, perfume, air freshener to hide smell of smoke or drugs.
- Using eyedrops to mask bloodshot eyes and dilated pupils.

Psychological warning signs of alcohol or drug abuse

- Unexplained, confusing change in personality and/or attitude.
- Sudden mood changes, irritability, angry outbursts or laughing at nothing.
- Periods of unusual hyperactivity or agitation.
- Lack of motivation; inability to focus, appears lethargic or "spaced out."
- Appears fearful, withdrawn, anxious, or paranoid, with no apparent reason.

Take these steps to monitor and confront your teen's substance use:

★ **Observe:** Many of the above warning signs, in isolation, can be misinterpreted. The first time your teenager has bloodshot eyes, is tired, seems withdrawn, does not necessarily mean that they have a problem with drugs or alcohol. But, they should be noted. As a parent, you have unmatched access to their everyday habits. You can see their behaviors like few can. This access and information comes with tremendous responsibility. Heighten your observation skills by reviewing the above markers and comparing them to your teenager. What do you notice? What has changed? What strikes a chord with you? It's easy to write them off, just as I said earlier, and treat them as disconnected dots. But, the more you observe, the more you will know: is there a larger problem that needs to be confronted?

★ **Journal:** Keeping a dated record of your teenager will help you discern fact from fiction. I recommend keeping a journal for a minimum of 30 days, and that 30 days needs to be within a typical sample of their life (try to avoid doing it over a vacation, with new variables). As you observe your teenager, a key next step is to track your observations in a simple, clear, and unemotional manner. I know when I go to the doctor for a cold or back issue one piece of information needed right out the gate is my symptoms—not only what they are, but their duration and severity. Journaling your observations can be critical in frontloading your medical professionals with vital information regarding your teen's substance issues, if that becomes the case.

★ **Compare:** After completing your observations, reflect on the totality of your sample month. Compare your journal to the above suggestion from the NCADD and look for patterned and consistent markers.

★ **Consult:** If you feel that there are enough markers to warrant alarm, take your journal and consult with a professional.

This might be a pediatrician, therapist trained in addiction, or even a school nurse. Based on your consultation with that professional, if still warranted, confront your teen.

★ **Confront:** Confronting teenagers is tricky. It can often end in an explosive situation resulting in heavy denial and anger from the confronted party. Before you confront your teen, write and organize your concerns; putting them in writing will be more powerful than verbally unloading on them. The confrontation must come from a place of love and concern, and avoid appearances of a *gotcha!* Treat it like a medical issue and not a free-will and teenager defiance standpoint. After all, addiction is a disease.

Avoid saying: You have a drug problem!

Instead, try saying: I am concerned with some of your patterns of behavior and want to discuss them with you.

Avoid saying: You get drunk every weekend and I know you're smoking weed!

Instead, try saying: I wanted to show you some observations I made over the past month and get your perspective on them.

You can see this sample template:

★ **Observation:** what behavior, sign or symptom you noticed

★ **Pattern:** how often you tracked the behavior, sign or symptom (with dates and examples for each)

★ **Connection to the NCADD list:** how their behavior, sign or symptom correlated with the professional warning signs

★ **Why it concerns their medical professional:** relay any pertinent information noted during your consultation

★ **Why it concerns you:** come from a place of love and concern for their health, vibrancy, and welfare.

Potential teenager response: I don't party that often.

Counter with: That's an interesting perspective. According to my observations, over the last month you ....

Potential teenager response: I can't believe you've been watching me, and talking to my doctor, I thought you trusted me!

Counter with: Because I love you, and trusted you, I didn't want to jump to conclusions or assume things without making sure my intuition was correct. Again, this isn't about being in trouble, it's about being healthy and living a long, successful life.

Potential teenager response: You're totally overreacting! None of my friend's parents act like this. You're crazy.

Counter with: I understand that you are surprised by this, but I'm not. I consulted with your doctor and a therapist before speaking with you to make sure that I wasn't out of line or over-reacting. As for your friends' parents, I'm not in charge of them, or their kids. I'm in charge of you, and because I love you, we're going to address this issue.

Disclaimer: The steps to confronting your teenager are merely suggestions and intended for low-level circumstances. Please consult your doctor or a professional trained in interventions before you embark on this process, especially when you suspect or have knowledge of significant substance abuse.

PART 2

Technology as Social Currency

If you're reading this book, it's (hopefully) rooted in your efforts to be a life jacket for an adolescent (maybe it's your own son or daughter, or niece or nephew or student or neighbor) to make sure each teenager gets a shot to be who they are destined to be. Or maybe you're reading to better understand the Xs and Os of being a teenager today, as it relates to your scenario. One of the key ways that teens communicate and interact is through the virtual world of social media.

The sad truth: Augmentation is the new authenticity. Filter this. Forge that. Show well. Look like a sexy dog in a selfie here, buy the latest clothes you cannot truly afford there; vape this, chug that. Go with flow. Be chill; whatever it takes remain tucked neatly as a welcomed member of the *it-crowd* and well below the judgmental eyes and neighborhood whispers. Image-conscious personas appear both in the land of back yard barbeques and high school course selection. Evermore, parents and their teens alike, find themselves immersed in a swarm of pressure to do what others do, like what others like, be who others are, even when it doesn't feel right. At all. Keeping up with the latest reality television family or the suburban *it family* often mutes the internal voice of reason and morality, only to replace it with the emojis of conformity and line-toeing. Despite the defiant inner voice shouting swear words at you, all is done out of fear from being judged or ostracized. Nowhere is the sad plight of authenticity more evident than when examining the complicated world of teenagers: being one and parenting one.

The social media revolution: Within the dynamics of the smartphones and the 24/7 access to communication that comes with them, is the most transformative element within that world: social media. Social media platforms have transformed and revolutionized communication and the concept of having, making, keeping, being, and interacting with friends. And often, these platforms are painted as the big bad wolf; and we only focus on their negative aspects. I am an example of one who engages in cautionary tales of social media in my various articles and when coaching families and parents or presenting to school districts. I strongly believe that social media platforms come with their own set of positives and negatives, and these qualities can be exploited based on the level of education, accountability and training teenagers have surrounding them. In short, when used correctly, social media platforms outperform any other option in terms of easy messaging. And of course, the opposite it true. When used for bad, evil, negativity, etc., those same platforms can outperform alternatives in the instant and sustained impact they can bestow on teenagers.

Social media is not a teenager-only problem: I am an avid user of social media, like many other adults. I am not an authenticity expert or snob; many aspects to my life are inauthentic. My Instagram handle, for example, is littered with pictures of various aspects of my personal and professional life. Now that in and of itself isn't necessarily fake or fraudulent; but it's the fact that they are posted after a ritual of being painstakingly filtered with Ludwig or Crema or Juno, and subsequently captioned and #hashtaged, that helps to advance the perception of their contextual perfection. I'm thirty-eight years old and feel pressure to filter my family photos; I sympathize with the immense pressure teenagers feel to advance the notion that their life is a floating cloud of artsy, sexy, sarcastic, or athletic perfection. The struggle is real, as they say.

Before we dig into this chapter, I urge you to take a few minutes and go on your own social media feeds. I'm not bashing social media; it is a powerful and much-needed channel of engagement and community. Right now, it's the most relevant, cross-generational medium out there. But, as you scroll through your various feeds, you might begin to see why it's so challenging to be a teenager today, and why it requires full investment to fully parent children today. Just scroll.

Doesn't everyone look perfect? And if they don't, isn't it because they're being shamed in some capacity? Not only are teenagers today influenced by their direct peer-to-peer relationships, but they are also by every other user with their artsy, sexy, sarcastic, or athletic feeds, many of which are posted by adults my age. Lord have mercy. Feeling ambitious? Take a gander at your own teen's feed. Scroll and reflect. There's a world of assumptions, projections, suggestions, information, judgement, and pressure being thrown every time they refresh their feeds.

Let your own observations drive important conversations with your teenager:

★ What types of posts or content irritate you? Why?

★ What assumptions do you make from others' posts?

★ What contrasts can you find between how your friends present themselves on social media versus what you know is (in reality) going on with them?

With social media, choose education instead of abstinence: It's better to teach them how to use it thoughtfully, morally, and wisely, than to preclude its use. Social media, when used correctly, is a useful tool. But it requires moderation, monitoring, and a firmly defined moral compass and family-defined terms of acceptable use policy.

Why education is best: Like anything else, when used with good intentions and care, social media has benefits. It's an excellent networking tool, source of real-time information and news, and provides an avenue to maintain and foster long-lasting relationships. As a parent, you can produce and groom your teen to become an adult ready to navigate the real world with finesse and grit. In the same way adults prepare student drivers for the road through practice, patience, and regulation, so too should adults and parents be mindful to the process of carefully layering in access and free-range to these platforms.

Critical aspects to address when discussing social media use:

★ **Who to follow:** Those you follow reflect your value system and public persona. Who you follow can usurp what you yourself post; for it will appear you agree with what others post through the validation given to them by your follows, likes, comments, etc.

★ **Appropriate posts:** Your posts are breadcrumbs of character. They create a virtual resume of priorities, activities, goals, social behaviors, employability, college admit-ability, etc.

★ **What to like, share, repost:** What you validate or champion with your likes, follows, shares, reposts speak volumes about your character and priorities.

★ **Role of the sideline accomplice:** Cyberbullying (which we'll look at in more detail later) is a spectator sport. Passively encouraging negative or aggressive behaviors with likes or mean posts yields elevated risk of being pulled into the matter when school or legal consequences come to fruition.

★ **Privacy settings:** To mitigate the risk of becoming prey for predatorial trolls on the Internet and social media, keeping your cards close to your vest is key. Maintaining a public profile takes tremendous responsibility of keeping the feed free of vulgar or inappropriate content. More so, do you want your every move to be seen by any potential cyber-stalker or antagonist, or college admissions counselor, or employer?

★ **Being the same person behind the screen as the one across the table:** Teens (and adults) commonly experience a distinct personality shift behind the screen or keyboard. What you say on a post, in a comment, send in a text—will forever come back to haunt you in the form of accountability. Make sure that the person you are at school and the person you are on the keys is in sync.

★ **The permanence of content posted:** Even when harmful content is wiped from social media platforms, it remains forever in the form of screenshots. Typically, when content lands a student in trouble, it is after someone has provided such images to officials. Many platforms thrive on disappearing content, but content only disappears when all viewers agree to and comply with allowing it to drift into the abyss.

Technological abstinence is not a winning approach: Phones, technology, social media, and newer concepts like artificial intelligence are not going to disappear. In fact, their footprint will only increase and become more substantial and mainstream over time. Instilling technological literacy and digital citizenship should be priorities as a parent. I'll address digital citizenship shortly, but first let's look at technological literacy.

Technological literacy is:

✓ Understanding how to use devices (smartphones, tablets, computers).

✓ Developing proper appreciation for the power and responsibility that accompanies use of such devices.

✓ Becoming well-versed in the valuable tools and software available.

✓ Gaining and honing marketable and transferrable skills that drive success in college and the workplace.

Stop and reflect with these questions:

What, if any, social media platforms do you use? Self-education is a valuable tool when understanding the machine of social media attachment and addiction. If you notice that you are not using any, the disconnect therein will make it hard to understand or appreciate the nuance, influence, and appeal to its use. If you do use them, reflecting on what emotions it creates within your own framework, as an adult, will clue you in to some of the exponential effects it has on teens. If you are already social media literate, dial into that literacy. For certain circumstances, it might be best to follow and engage with your teen on the platform; in others, it might be better to know how they work, and simply use that knowledge to drive conversations regarding propriety of use.

How much time you spend on these platforms per day? Leading by looking within is a critical skill for adults to embrace when managing teenager behavior. If you find yourself constantly attached to your smartphone, computer, or tablet, engaged in tracking down the latest posts, commenting, sharing, liking, etc., then you have a bit of the same addictive qualities as many users. Teenagers do not respond well when you are seeking actions from them that you yourself are not living. Undoubtedly, with things like alcohol, you have a legality to forward your directives; but with social media and technology use, you don't.

How much stock to you put into your posts? Are you sensitive to the response and feedback that you receive from your posts? Do you get excited when a new user likes your post? Do you censor your posts to project a specific type of reputation or footprint or social position on the Internet? Teenagers place a high value on the feedback, or lack of feedback, they receive. But in my own reflection, it's safe to say, so do I. It's normal to want validation; but for teenagers, who lack confidence and are uncertain of their true self, their posts are how they communicate, and are considered social currency.

Who within your network are you "friends" with or follow yet don't really know; or know, but don't like? This is true of me. I'll admit it. Specifically, with old "friends" that I went to high school with. I get a request, thinking, "You must remember our relationship differently than I do." Social media relationships sometimes don't feel optional: it's more of an opt-out system. Be friends with everyone and then block, unfollow, or delete them when they wrong you. That is very much the social media structure for teenagers: the more friends and followers the better. Again, that is their social currency, and a defining stat when understanding the teenager popularity hierarchy.

Why social media is so intoxicating for teenagers:
✓ It creates a sense of connection.

✓ It keeps them in the know.

✓ It provides them validation with likes, reposts, comments and followers.

✓ It makes them feel included.

✓ It allows them to present the optics of their lives on their own terms.

Why social media can be damaging for teenagers:
✓ It exacerbates their lack of connection.

✓ It highlights what they didn't know (in a bad way).

✓ It makes them feel marginalized and unimportant.

✓ It makes them feel excluded or subjects them to bullying and aggression.

✓ It creates an inescapable pressure to exude perfection and happiness that is many times, absent.

Activity: Social Media Awareness

Directions: Identify which social media or communication platforms your teenagers use and their handle (username) if you know it (ex: @pattersonperspective).

Instagram   _____

Finsta   _____

Facebook   _____

Snapchat   _____

Twitter   _____

YouTube   _____

Kik   _____

Tumbler   _____

WhatsApp   _____

Venmo   _____

Email   _____

Xbox Live   _____

A quick reflection:

★ How many of these social media platforms were you able to identify?

★ Which platforms do you use?

★ Examine the platforms on which you follow your teenager.

★ Are there any you have never heard of?

Be informed: Not understanding how social media works, or how to download it on your phone is very much a choice at this point. There are too many tools, YouTube videos, and even consultants available to you to remain ignorant of the platforms. While you may not like social media, or even prefer not to use it, it is important that you heighten your awareness to this very dominant part of your teen's life.

Take initiative with these steps:

✓ Identify the social media platforms your teen is using.

✓ Create an account and friend or follow your teenager.

✓ Use an alias if needed to save face for your teen (their friends won't know it's you).

✓ Utilize the tips and tutorials within the platforms to better understand how they work.

✓ Monitor, but don't stalk.

Monitor at your own pace: Now there are proponents of high and tight monitoring via third party applications and software (parental spyware, in essence). I have mixed feelings on those. It's a case-by-case basis, and lives in the world of *you can't un-see what you'll see.* Not to suggest that you carry on as an ignorant parent, only to say that you don't need to, nor would you really benefit from, knowing about all searches on your son's smartphone. I refrain from making an overarching recommendation either way; what I do recommend, though, is knowing what your options are in terms of said services and having a pre-established understanding in terms of implementation for scenarios that teens create for their parents.

Although I don't make a clear directive in terms of subscription-based monitoring, I will openly tell you to regularly spot check and indirectly monitor their use on said phones and social media platforms. The two main concerns that I know to be relevant to teenagers today are cyber-bullying and dark web temptations. Cyber-bullying, of course, is well-hyped and somewhat overexposed. Parents need to look for signs that their child is either cyberbullying (most common) or being cyberbullied (slightly less common). Parents are more likely to discover (hopefully in disappointment and shock) that their teen is acting as an aggressor online.

Examples of Red Flags:

✓ Your teen is being subjected to cyberbullying or cyber-aggression.

✓ Your teen is subjecting others to cyberbullying or cyber-aggression.

✓ Your teen is taking, sending, or receiving explicitly sexual images or video clips.

✓ Your teen is communicating with someone you have never heard of, don't know, or who your teen has been directed to stay away from.

✓ Your teen is sending or receiving large or frequent amounts of money via apps like Venmo.

✓ Your teen continuously turns off their location services on their device.

Social media platforms have evolved to be elusive: Preferred teenage social media platforms thrive on their ability to disappear and dissolve. For example, the third-party software systems sold to parents are great for tracking Internet activity, monitoring app use and downloads, and even providing the ability to read text messages and emails. However, teenagers are aware of this and have moved conversations and messaging to avenues where tracking and monitoring is basically impossible (unless you have the device in your hand). For this reason, arming your teen with a well-defined moral compass and awareness regarding appropriate use is far more impactful than any sort of big brother approach.

Your rights and responsibilities: If you pay for the iPhone, the Apple ID, the cloud, etc., then you have the right to know what's on the device. With the Apple ID there are various "big brother" programs that you can sync with the device, which will track all activity. Does this mean you have to read it all? Please don't. You can't un-see what you might see ... however, it is good to check in and monitor for warning signs. Plenty of vendors and software exist at this point that it is purely chosen ignorance not to know what your teen is doing on or with their smartphone.

A connection better acknowledged than ignored: The advent, evolution and integration of the smartphone into the fold of mainstream society has without question changed the modern world. This is not the time nor the place to debate the benefits of this integration, but this is an appropriate time to appropriately acknowledge the power and direct impact the smartphone has on our teenager's daily lives and their sense of self-identity. Teenagers view the smartphone as a direct extension of their being; with it they feel empowered, connected, and find meaning in ways that adults don't always understand.

Technology is a constant in their lives: Teenagers today were in many ways born with a phone, or tablet of some kind in their hands. This separation of paradigmatic reality is vital to notice. The adults in their lives at some point lived a life with a stark contrast in terms of the technologies they had access to and could afford, and the platforms on these devices that make interaction so seamless today. I remember my first cellphone. It was purchased in 2001 after I graduated from college. A sleek Nokia phone, with Cingular wireless, complete with a bill that was over-the-top expensive, and void of any features except thumb-intensive texting and old-fashioned phone calls. Basically, it was a glorified pager. Prior to that purchase, I had slummed it with modes of communication like emails compliments of dial-up and keeping a pre-paid calling card in my pocket to use in cases of *this conversation cannot wait until I get back to my landline.* A landline. Can you imagine if your teenagers had to wait to communicate by either logging on to their email via dial-up and a desktop computer or on your phone in that office area in the kitchen? The comedy. It's examples like these that really highlight the generational divide that technology has created.

Smartphones and driver's licenses are very similar.

Driver's License and Smartphones

Provide tremendous freedoms

Carry tremendous responsibility

Allow for risky and dangerous situations

Are powerful possessions in teens' lives

Smartphones are given without much forethought and preparation for their teen users, while driver's licenses are more appropriately regulated.

Driver's License	Smartphone
Multiple written tests required	No test required
Age of use strictly enforced	Age of use rarely enforced
Mandatory studying and practice required	No preparation or studying required
Heavily regulated safety procedures in place	Rarely regulated
Graduated access with age and practice	One size fits all access
Mistakes have well-defined consequences	Mistakes are left up to parents to manage

Tips for introducing a smartphone

★ **Less is more to begin:** You can't put toothpaste back into the tube. The longer you wait to issue your first smartphone to your (pre)teenager the better. When you do issue the first one, it does not have to be the latest, fully loaded, model. Start with a phone that can browse online, call, and text. Those are all easily monitored.

★ **Heavily regulate its use early, and back off over time:** Like the way teens traverse the process of obtaining their permit and license (which carry set markers, proof of acceptable abilities and responsibility) so, too, can you apply those types of systems to your teen's smartphone use and access. Don't wait until there is an issue to monitor and regulate; make them earn their way to access and autonomy. Habits formed early in their use will be more effective and maintainable than trying to create new habits after making a big mistake.

★ **Integrate social media platforms in accordance with your ability to monitor use:** This goes along with the type of phone you provide them. Many teens lobby for a phone with vast capabilities. Included in those capabilities are the phone's ability to support social media platforms. The social media platforms that operate within margins you can properly or more easily monitor should be granted first. Platforms promoting secrecy should be implemented last.

Obligation to educate and create boundaries: Smartphones are wonderful in that they provide communities access to 24/7 communication, real time information and provide the ability to remain connected to the world regardless of one's location (assuming you have WiFi or bars). This kind of wonderful, though, is the kind that cuts both ways. Widely accepted research clearly confronts the reality that the teenage brain is unable to manage many logistical functions such as moderation, risk analysis, impulse control, and long-term planning. This is not to say that teenagers cannot learn to implement these types of decision-making skills in their lives with the help of training, good role models, and accountability; but it is a reminder that we need to remember that big bodies and mature physical features should not be, but frequently are, confused for mental maturity. Translation: adults need to assert measures into the lives of teenagers that help them understand and manage the power, proximity, and potential (both good and bad) of their devices.

Smartphones are powerful access points: You will be hard pressed to find a more powerful device, tool, resource, etc., on the planet as small, accessible, and commonly used as a smartphone. And that small size can be misleading. Many parents overlook the wide variety of content and information that accompany these devices. They provide access to so much content, good and bad, innocent and obscene, and it's easy to forget that. I understand that many families implement rules or guidelines in their homes associated with phones. A common example is one where once the child turns a specific age they automatically get a phone. Depending on social pragmatics and economics, that age can be as old as twelve and as young as six. Six. I know. But I can see how we can get there in a hurry. My own children were fully capable of using the iPads in our home by the age of two. So, my three-year-old daughter is scrolling through Netflix looking for a new episode of Barney and my sixty-something-year-old mother is handing me the same device because it's locked. Again, generational divide (sorry, Mom. Now within the handing-off of devices there are a variety of techniques that can be used to monitor, control, and reduce access on them, but those measures are primarily bumpers, or Band-Aids, and do not address the actual concern at hand, which is digital citizenship.

Benefits of the powerful access point:

✓ Increased autonomy and independence

✓ Your teen is always reachable

✓ Increased engagement with peers and others on social media

✓ Your teen is better prepared in the event of an emergency

Downside of the powerful access point:

✓ Your teen may experience a substantial increased pull into the social fold

✓ Your teen is always reachable

✓ Your teen may be more vulnerable to manipulation and exploitation

✓ Your teen many be more likely to experience an actual emergency

Tips to managing phones

★ **Park the phones in your bedroom:** Teenagers lack impulse control. Really though, the battle with technology compulsion is a human problem. Teenagers cannot help themselves but to use the device that is next to their bed. Sleep is crucial to teenage health and vibrancy. Research suggests that the phone can disrupt sleep purely based on the light it emits. On a practical level, the phone keeps them connected and disallows them to unplug and withdraw into themselves to rest and reset. Another bonus is that the fact that you will have the device in your room will inherently decrease the low-key sketchy behavior on the device when they do have it with them. Bonus!

★ **Identify a phone-free period for academics:** Without fail, one of the first strategies employed by teens when you take or limit their phone use, is that they *need* it for school work. I'll give this a 50% accuracy rating. What they mean, is that they rely on it for quick information such as assignments, grades, and interacting with their peers during work completion for help and collaborative efforts. The phone is the number one efficiency killer of student studying: it has significantly more negatives than the positive of quick information. Students can gather their needed information prior to beginning their studies. If they need their phone to do this, allow them a grace period of 10 minutes to gather that information, or simply provide them use of the family computer, which is in plain sight. If you commit to weening your teen off the phone while they study, you will see an increase in progress. It's undeniable.

★ **Use your phone provider's available parent control features:** Phone providers have easy-to-use systems in place that allow you to limit your teen's accessibility to apps and even data (Internet). This is a great option if you simply don't want to take the phone away during studying. This move is more symbolic than practical. There are work-arounds to most parent big-brother type moves, but the more you try to monitor and help limit the phone's use, the less likely they are to end up severely abusing the device or using it for ill. Unfortunately, many parents don't take advantage of such technology until they are given a reason. I get it, you want to trust your teen, but we don't require teens to only take driver's education if they get into an accident. I support the concept of a gradual release. It's far easier to start with firm supports in place, and then to gradually ease out of them with evidence of good habits and use.

★ **Embrace phone-free dining:** I'm not going to spend a lot of time on this one. It's simple. When you are eating together, or they are eating a meal, no phone. The phone is an isolative device within the home. Yes, it establishes their sense of connection to others outside the home; but in the true sense, it serves as a communicative and relational barrier. That means no phones for parents, either. No work calls, no Googling, nothing. Just old fashioned awkward silence and family conversation. The more you do it, the easier it will be, as it becomes the one reprieve from their habitual use.

★ **Use them as the motivator that they are:** Phones really are the golden ticket with most teens. It is far more powerful than you might realize, or they will even admit. Many teenagers don't know how to navigate socially without one, which is further proof that they truly only know life with the smartphone as an extension of their being. Phones should be treated as a true privilege and only given to those who can comply with family directives and goals. I'm not saying to take it at every turn, but know that it is very powerful in the motivation game. Parents tend to worry that taking the phone further complicates their own parenting: not being able to reach them, etc. You did it, and so can they.

Group chats are the new lunch tables: One reason phones are such powerful motivational tools, and why teenagers are attached to them, is a result of group chats. Social status and friend groups were once easily defined by where students sat at lunch. While this is still true today, with the shape of schools with schedules and busy kids moving in every which direction, it isn't as reliable a measure as it once was. Today, you are much more likely to find a huge mass of students sitting together, eating, and interacting with their group chat. A group chat defines a friend group. No group chat, no friends. That's how it's viewed by teenagers, anyhow.

Group chats: Group chats are simply group text messages that populate into a single, and exclusive list. Teenagers post and interact all day and night long with the group.

Layers upon layers: Teenagers are often engaged in multiple group chats. Imagine a target, with the largest outer layer representing an entire, large, peer group. And then within that there are smaller circles, representing the more intimate or exclusive sub-groups therein. There might be a co-ed group chat, and within that same group, one for each gender, and then within those, smaller ones. I recently learned of a group chat of high school students that existed entirely to prompt the members to like and comment on new social media posts. The peers were not all friends, but rather, were social allies.

Diverse purposes: You will discover group chats evolve for specific classes, where students can ask classmates questions about due dates, for help on an assignment, or to vent about the teacher. There are others that simply organize events like bus groups for school dances or teams to maintain cohesive communication regarding practice and game times.

Why they matter: Group chats, like many other items discussed in this book, serve as social currency. A group chat signifies that your teenager has found their people. Group chats are signals of social hierarchy and status. They can be hard to find and easy to lose. Social lives crumble when they get ejected from a group chat. They no longer exist within the very valuable virtual life stream.

How they work: Group chats work to maintain and restore social order. Typically, an alpha peer, or peers, creates the group and selects those to invite. Once invited, the invitees work very hard to stay in the group, and are careful not to defy or disrupt the alpha peer(s). I've worked with teenagers who have articulated that their primary social goal was to earn an invitation to a specific group chat. For example, they would eat with, hang out with, study with members of the chat, in their efforts to get "in."

Digital citizenship: Digital citizenship is a big buzzword in educational technology conversation and has been for quite some time. And parents are referring to it all the time, only they aren't always aware of it. Digital citizenship is the set of ethical rules and responsibilities that dictate, or drive expected or responsible use as dictated by institutions (such as schools) or within the family unit. Practically, in the school setting we see this commonly with rules associated with phone use on campus: can they have them out, or not, if so, when, etc.

Common technology-related school integrity infractions:

✓ Unauthorized collaboration, in real time, with just a few keystrokes

✓ Photographing and distributing test or quiz questions and answers

✓ Sharing assignments

✓ Plagiarizing

✓ Not really reading their novel

✓ Purchasing a pre-written essay online

While we as digitally-divided adults see this as a clear and crisp beacon of obviousness, the teenagers do not possess that paradigm. We see phones and view them as a shortcut from *looking it up* or *using an Encyclopedia*. Teens will ask, *Encylopedi-what?!* So digital citizenship requires education, and that process requires work. The concept of digital citizenship, while now implemented as a proactive measure in places like school, is still very much reactionary or missing altogether in the framework of technology within the home.

Common home-related integrity infractions:

✓ Viewing pornography

✓ Communicating with friends outside acceptable timeframes

✓ Communication with peers/adults they should not be in communication with

✓ Using social media platforms without permission

✓ Using ride-sharing apps without permission

✓ Recording images or videos of family members and posting it on social media or group chats

✓ Inappropriately communicating with peers from home (cyber bullying, sexting)

Cyberbullying: Teenage cyberbullying is a spectator sport. Teenagers typically team up to rely on a strength-in-numbers approach; this approach allows them to strategically alienate, humiliate, or deflate another peer without having to be solely responsible for said actions. Of course, there are degrees of culpability within the arena of cyberbullying

Cyber-harassment in real life: I was once harassed for a good six months by webmasters of an anonymous social interaction site used by teenagers to vent and confess their transgressions, regressions, and often entertaining antics. Now mind you, this was a vast network, extending across all social media options, with thousands and thousands of users and followers. They would post on my social media, and know where I was, mock me, say mean things, and attempt to hack into my feed while egging on others to do the same. Outwardly I held it together well, presenting that it was not bothering me. Inwardly, though, it resurrected old and deeply guarded feelings associated with being bullied. The experience was absolutely excruciating at times, although, in the end, it was an amazing learning experience. I was living what the kids at my high school lived every day; I was the victim of cyberbullying. I will use the term victim lightly here; there were no threats to my safety and after all, it was just kids. The hardest part was not knowing who they were. I understood why: I was an easy target. A school administrator, with a strong social media presence, who was all over the place. I was not typical. I was in plain view, and created it that way on purpose, and this was a side effect of that. Nonetheless, it was a blessing: I imagined that the emotions I was experiencing in reaction to their cyber antics were only the tip of the iceberg compared to the reactions from teenagers going through similar interactions online.

I did my due diligence and put forth my best effort to uncover the culprits. And the fact that they came after me personally meant they knew me, and I knew them, at least to some degree. Ultimately, once I decided to find the culprit, it only took about one month to find the trail leading straight to the webmaster's campus asset, which in turn led me to the head honcho. I swear this sounds like a movie, but it was my real life. Each school had representatives that fed intel and confessions and dirt to the webmasters, who in turn used them on their feed.

Now, while I won't ever reveal the source of the leak, I can tell you that the source had no idea they were the source. The main strategy I used when finding out the webmaster's identity was the same one I used in most of my intel work: listening. I will repeat that listening is the most underutilized technique used in adult-to-teen communication. Adults, quite frankly, don't listen to teenagers. Sometimes, most times actually, the disconnect between teenagers and adults is the lack of equilibrium in the listening department.

The source first came into my office in complete dismay, having been denied acceptance to the college of their dreams; this was a student I had taught as a 7th grader, and I knew I wanted to help. In our meeting, much trauma was flushed out: home life, social stressors, teacher conflicts, and a whole lot of academic effort-related regret. The session ended with a rough appeal plan effort and a follow-up meeting with the student's mother.

The following day the student's parent came in to follow up. Again, listening was my primary technique. After similar sentiments regarding the student's setbacks and regrets, we focused on the appeal plan. The plan, taken somewhere from *Legally Blonde* and nextgen thinking, was to create an Instagram account for the student, which was strictly meant to market their strengths and devotion to the prospective college. We brainstormed post ideas and the overall appeal process. And then, boom. A bomb dropped.

"This is such a good idea! After all, (student name) is so good at social media! (S)he even runs that page. You know, the confessions one."

Bingo.

To this day, I'm still not sure if the parents knew they blew the cover, or if they ever told their child that the secret had been revealed. At the next meeting with the student, we discussed the plan in detail. Posts. New letters of recommendation, including one from me. This is where the Jekyll and Hyde of teenage social media use became crystallized. Here was a student who I had helped, who I had a positive relationship with, had known, etc., for six years. And one side of them sought my help in appealing their college denials, while the other side of them harassed me online, or at least knew who did, and hadn't stopped it.

"I'm really excited by this idea, thank you," they said. "I love social media!"

"Yes, I think it might just work. Especially since you have the experience of running a large social media site. This should be easy," I replied with a steady and unemotional tone.

I will never forget the size of their eyes, or the speed with which the blood drained from their face. A few weeks later their appeal was granted, and I never heard from the webmasters again.

Sometimes, all you must do is listen.

A case study in cyberbulling via social media: *Finsta; noun; a fake (or second) Instagram account; primarily used to hide scandalous and overtly sexual behavior, cultivate an alter ego, and function with anonymity to troll peers.*

The Finsta phenomenon began the moment parents invaded Facebook ... and subsequently Instagram. Prior to being usurped by this mid-40s, iPad-wielding force, teens independently occupied the open channels of social media. Chronicles of debauchery, sexy outfits, best-dinners-ever, hookups, breakups, politics, road trips, beach days, and everything in between were documented by a plethora of openly and unabashedly flaunted pictures and videos. But as more parents began "friending" and "following" and "posting," so, too, declined the allure of these channels for teens; the platforms once synonymous with freedom, became not so free. Teenagers faced a choice: quit social media or evolve. They chose evolution ... in the form of Finstas.

The birth of the Finsta can be traced to the time between the generational hijacking of Facebook and Instagram, but before the adoption of SnapChat. While the Finsta phenomenon is old news to teenagers, it continues to wreak havoc on their lives. Regardless, teenagers can't seem to shake the Finsta.

Originally born from the desire to carve out a space free from nosey parents, Finstas have morphed into an animal capable of reducing even the most well-adjusted teens to rubble.

Finsta facts:

✓ The world of Finsta is heavily dominated by teenage users.

✓ Finsta handles (or names) are sexually explicit or suggestive and somehow weave in the creator's actual name.

✓ A Finsta's creator can be traced by an experienced Finstigator by analyzing the Finsta's followers, posts, and respective reactions and interactions (likes, comments, regrams).

✓ Finstas often intentionally cross paths with Rinstas (real Instagrams) to launch social media cyber assaults and stir calm waters.

✓ Finstas are the preferred platform for teens to methodically humiliate, ostracize, and bully their peers.

Finsta realities:

✓ Most teenagers at some point have a Finsta (although they will deny, deny, deny).

✓ It is more common to have a Finsta, than to not have a Finsta.

✓ Finstas begin with good intentions; however most ultimately are used to engage in either direct cyber aggression, or sideline encouragement of the aggressive antics of others.

✓ Finstas that create mental, social, or emotional trauma are subject to school-related discipline if and when they bleed into the school environment.

✓ Upon discovery, teens easily (and alarmingly) convince parents the Finsta is "only a joke" or "actually never used," and quickly change their handle (name) to advance the illusion that it is gone.

Finsta dangers:

✓ Most teenagers will at some point experience the wrath of a Finsta bully or bullies.

✓ Even the most level-headed and socially responsible teens eventually succumb to the temptation to use their Finsta as a tool of immorality.

✓ Finstas never actually go away. Yes, they can be deleted or buried, but screenshots and recovery measures make content live on forever.

✓ Cyber-bullying is currently one of the hottest topics in teenagedom, with all eyes on Finstas; the odds of the creator's eventual exposure are significantly higher than even a year ago.

✓ Finstas expose users to the underbelly of deviance where all things inappropriate are not only encouraged, but expected as a baseline standard of use.

Finstas have become the Wild West of social media: the only rule is that there are no rules; couple that with (perceived) anonymity, angst, sexual curiosity, envy, insecurity, relationships, and rivalry, and you have entered the world of Finsta. The world of Finsta is fun, until it isn't; you're anonymous, until you aren't; they're harmless, until they're malicious; and they have no impact, until their blunt force trauma takes you out at the knees.

The technologically-hyped sexual subculture of high school: High schoolers think they know what is, and what isn't. And they generally live within those realities. They see black and white; they don't do well with grey. This is applicable to rules within the household and academics—but also in the way they view each other in the social realm.

Constant classification: Teens quickly classify each other into many social sub-categories, placing each acquaintance within the basic shell of who they think will, and will not do the following:

✓ Drink with me.

✓ Vape with me.

✓ Sext with me.

✓ Hook up with me.

✓ Send me naked pics.

✓ Be trusted not to share these actions with others.

Teens often draw their conclusions from content posted to social media feeds, pulling indicators from visual cues, like outfits worn or activities documented and celebrated. Again, it's vital to appreciate that within social media, teens are exposed to adults being adults, doing what adults do—creating a desire to be, act, dress, and do as the adults are doing.

Sexting: Sexting, if you are not aware of the term, is the exchange of naked or nude photos between two parties, or explicit and graphic words depicting sexual activity, and in many cases, both. This may be a mutual exchange, where one party sends one to the other, and vice versa. It also may be a one-sided affair, with only one recipient.

Origins and influences of sexting: Technology plays a huge role in the rising tide of the over-sexualization-of-teenagers phenomenon; it has become increasingly and alarmingly ingrained into the fiber of the teenage microculture. Specifically, social media is now a primary avenue where teenagers are far too often exploited, and subsequently victim-shamed in the process. Exploitation and shaming can range from direct to subtle as teens are manipulated by each at lightning speed.

Is social media to blame? This is a complicated question, in a chicken-egg sort of way. Some believe social media is not the culprit, merely the messenger of tendencies and behaviors that were always there; today they're simply more obvious and easy to find or distribute through social media platforms. Others have the opposite stance: technology, and social media, significantly elevated and accelerated teenage behaviors and tendencies. Teenagers who are overexposed to social media from an early age become programmed to a way of thinking that aligns suggestive or regrettable posts, actions, and messages, with normal and acceptable behavior.

Blame the example: Many of the social media that are most preferred or followed by teenagers are led by a pack of overly-suggestive, nearly-naked, or naked-naked celebrities and other influencers. Part of the image or persona of these highly sought after, highly paid individuals, is their reliance solely on suggestive tones as a key ingredient in their branding. These savvy influencers know exactly what they are doing within their larger brand management campaign. Get paid to post? Yes, please! However, easily impressionable and socially fragile young teenagers see these and copycat posts by the hundreds or thousands, daily, for years. Can we honestly expect them not to fall in line and begin posting them as well?

Nude pics as social currency: Modeling the behaviors of their idols' ever-present, social-influencer force, curious teenagers then look for work towards establishing their own high school brand, with an extensive social media following; sometimes they extend their sexually suggestive tones into their peer-to-peer communication in what is known as sexting. Sharing naked and suggestive pictures generates buzz, interest, and gossip—all which work (until they don't) to elevate their social status with peers.

Who sexts? In short, everyone is eligible. I have regrettably known far too many young teens from varying family structures, economic realities, friend groups, GPA ranges, sports, faith back-grounds etc. that at some point sent or received a naked picture or sexually explicit message.

Why they do it?

★ **Curiosity:** Teenagers are curious beings. They see much on the Internet, but long to see it for themselves via someone they know. They are curious about their own social currency—what can they, in their present social status, get from others? How much does their pressure deliver? On the flip side of the coin, many who send the images are curious of where it will get them socially. Into a relationship with a person who likes them? Attention? Social buzz?

★ **Pressure:** Teenagers are socially compliant beings who cave under the pressures of social norms and expected behaviors. Many arrive to a place requesting or sending images by rep-resenting their friend group in the act. Translation: multiple kids are on both sides of the conversation (sender/receiver) egging on and pressuring one token member in their group to do the act itself. For example, many of these transgressions occur at sleepovers (which is another good reason not to al-low sleepovers).

★ **Leverage:** Naked images are a powerful form of social cur-rency. When images leak to other peers, like onto group chats and social media, it's from a former friend or intimate part-ner (boyfriend, girlfriend, friend with benefits). Images are great tools when issuing passive or active threats against a friend who might reveal a secret, or a partner attempting to leave a relationship. The images themselves often keep kids in line, so to speak, as they operate out of retaliatory fear.

Collected: Teens have essentially begun collecting nudes like I collected baseball cards as a child. And I don't really think they all want to, either. I collected hundreds of baseball cards as a young teenager, and I didn't even really enjoy baseball; I did it because everyone else did. There was an undercurrent of pres-sure to do so, to fit in, and that was with baseball cards.

Not my kid! They would never ask someone to send a naked picture!
*gets called to principal's office two weeks later.

But, still, why? Obvious is the fact that teenagers engaging in sexting have been either manipulated into sending the images, or manipulated into believing that receiving one is an appropriate choice. This manipulation stems from peer-to-peer pressure, social norms, viewing the pictures as social currency, or having them leaked from their device by a spiteful ex-friend or partner.

Based on my experience in this topic (the interchange of nudes in the adolescent setting) about half the recipients really want them, and the other half feel pressure to collect them. Teenagers are essentially walking through a field of landmines. They have the headwind of social media influencers and celebrities, the pressure to conform to industry standards of pretty and sexy at school, and then the peers fawning all over them and manipulating them to send naked pictures. It's alarming.

Here's the sample progression I've witnessed time and again:
★ Peer identifies target.
★ Peers start Snapping, Insta-messaging, crushing on, stroking the ego.
★ Target is overwhelmed by the attention.
★ Peer leans in with more passion, more prose, and more hungry desperation.
★ Targets, against their better judgement, but clouded by the influx of subconscious validators (i.e., influencers' social media posts) send the nude photo.
★ Poof! Peer disappears into the cyber-space abyss.
★ Target is mortified as their picture is leaked to others in the teenage subculture.
★ Peer denies leaking image.
★ Peer somehow manipulates the situation to look like they're also a victim.

★ And maybe, in a sense, they are, if they're in the half of the pack that really doesn't want to be collecting these, but does anyhow, to conform.

★ Target is then criminalized as a slut or troublemaker by their ruthless peers.

★ People accuse Target of doing it for attention, which they weren't. Exactly. They were manipulated into it. And it's gross. They're the victim here.

As a parent, you are charged with the mission to help your children understand their self-worth within the context of a variety of situations. What is to be valued? How can they know that their value is real? Or lasting? How do they maintain the integrity of their value? Protect their value? How can they recover from a mistake? One of the biggest mistakes parents make is waiting until after an event of devaluation or exploitation, to help their teenagers understand their actual and full value as a human. Don't wait. Have the conversation. Knowledge is power.

Tips to combat or address sexting

★ **See something, say something:** If you notice your teen has or is discussing any kind of inappropriate messages, address the issue head-on. This is not the time to shy from conflict, or worry about calling another parent to inform them that their child has sent or received inappropriate messages. The earlier the issue is addressed, the less likely it is to hit the mainstream teenager feed.

★ **Instruct them to delete any images on their devices immediately if you discover them:** Don't suggest, or instruct: watch the images be deleted. This isn't about hiding involvement, it's about protecting them, and others, from the spread of such images and escalating the situation.

★ **Reinforce the ramifications and potential fallout from these images:** Be proactive and discuss the matter with your teenager. There are several serious outcomes that can accompany such messages such as suspension from school, police involvement, litigation from other families, and social alienation and exclusion. Planting seeds of consequence may lead to better choices in the future.

★ **Report any instance of an exchange to school officials who can better help cleanse them from others' phones:** Getting school officials involved might sound counterproductive, as the instance might not have taken place in school. However, schools have amazing leverage and abilities to cage-rattle to restore best practices. Many schools have school resource officers (police) who can also mediate and mitigate the spread of images without becoming involved on a legal level. Their presence is often enough to squash most scenarios.

★ **Understand the permanence of images:** Once an image has leaked in the high school setting, the probability of containment is high (based on school leverage, school resource officers and cooperation from other parents) but the probability of elimination is low (someone always keeps it, somewhere).

Confronting objectivity: Here in lies a major (yet often missed) opportunity for parents to educate their teenager on the importance of respecting others. This goes way beyond the context of school. It goes beyond the context of girl or boy; it's a human issue. Some people dress provocatively. Some people post suggestive content on social media. No one is going to change those. Parents should strive to make it clearly understood that dress or visual cues are not invitations for exploitation. While I appreciate school dress codes in their efforts to maintain a focused atmosphere, I also believe that people should dress however they please (on their own time) without being subjected to inappropriate or presumptuous behavior from anyone. Does that mean their parents should let them wear whatever they want? Maybe. That's up to the family value system, not me.

Staring sexual assault in the eyes: One growing concern in the high school and college setting (beyond the classroom) is the concept of sexual entitlement and the rape culture. Peers who think they somehow deserve or are entitled to another's body, when they are not; even when the peer is drunk; even when they are dressed a certain way. Whatever the case. It doesn't matter, so let's not criminalize the victim.

Empower your teenager: While I believe in freedom of expression, that freedom brings with it certain responsibilities to safeguard them. As a parent, if you empower your teenager to wear whatever they choose, please make sure that you are talking to them about the potential scenarios that may play out; and how to confidently combat negative, aggressive, assumptive or unwanted advances. Teens may unfairly assume that peers want to engage in sexual encounters. Or worse, they may ignore the peer's wants and needs altogether and assault them. When these things happen, what can, or should the victims do? What are the resources? Parents need to arm their teenagers with the understanding that while they have a choice to be and dress however they want, they need to own that choice by having a firm grip on who they are as a person, and defend that truth at all costs. They are not an object. End of conversation.

Set examples of authentic relationships: A friend of mine who has daughters, recently adopted the practice of a father-daughter date night. They get dressed up, and he takes them (individually) to do something fun; an activity or meal or experience, to not only show them what it's like to do something besides *hangout*, but also to subtly reinforce the way in which his daughters deserve to be treated. They are learning through experience what that feels like. It's more powerful than any car-ride lecture will ever be. I have a friend who is a single mother to multiple boys, who makes time with each one to have adventures and experiences that allow them to connect in healthy, active and positive ways. She is teaching her young men what it means to connect without the vibe of a party or tailgate and engage in meaningful conversation with an adult.

Managing the acceleration of teenage sexual behaviors: Little is more alarming to me now than the rise of sexy. Sex sells and is being developed for, sold to, and peddled by younger and younger consumers than ever before. Look at Halloween costumes. Every one of them is a provocative (fill in the blank). They are edgy and envelope-pushing. In teaching in the same place for years, I had a front row seat to the steep and hilarious (for all the wrong reasons) decline from creative costumes, to more seductive options. Sexy everything, all the time. To the point where kids were roaming the halls with their friends, all claiming *I'm a sexy gas station. I'm a sexy thermos.* Whatever it was, the more provocative the better.

It's just getting faster: I get it, I need to evolve with the times and get on board. Times-they-are-a-changing ... but holy cow, do the times have to be so image-obsessed? I'm waiting for the day when I go to pick up a new Lego set for my oldest daughter and find a sexy option as one of the choices. Maybe a sexy fire station, or a scantily-clad Plymouth Rock scene. Either way, time will tell. And while Halloween is only one day each year, it accurately and anecdotally summarizes the state of image-obsession and acceleration of adult behavior in schools. It represents the caravan of young people driving 100mph on the road to twenty-something.

School dress code: School dress code is one of the most polarizing topics right now. Are they needed? Warranted? Objectifying? A double standard? Out-dated? My thought is ... yes, to all. That's the dilemma. Without fail, a few times each year, a spattering of tone-deaf schools make national headlines because they got it wrong and sent home a student who dyed their hair purple or wore a Feel the Bern hat or something. Subsequently, the debate over school dress code rages hard for a few weeks, before decreasing back to a low smolder. But more often than not, dress code just kind of ebbs and flows through the teenage, high-school experience, as kids push the envelope while simultaneously conforming to so-and-so's latest line.

I, of course, as an assistant principal, had the privilege of dealing with this lovely process. In came a stream of "violators" sent to the office for wearing short-shorts, crop-tops, see-through-tops, marijuana hats, band t-shirts, sagging pants, etc. On a personal level, I didn't fully care what they were wearing, but in the interest of maintaining an academic setting, it was my job to enforce it. Most "violators" would begrudgingly change their clothes and return to class with a glare or mildly entertaining sarcastic comment. Once, even, a student locked themself inside the staff office bathroom and wouldn't come out until a parent arrived, at which point all hell broke loose. Upon arrival, the parent loudly accused me of objectifying the teen and left with tearful child in tow, promising to call the press.

The *you're objectifying my teenager* argument was very common, and caused lots of reflection as to whether dress codes, rather than allowing freedom of expression, really just made the problem worse. I, of course, never wanted to be part of a larger scale effort or system that objectified teens.

Angry Inappropriately Dressed Parent: *Well why did you even notice the way they dress? Are you some kind of pervert?*
Me: *(*silence)*

Is dress code equitable: In those moments, I was just doing my job, and disregarded such attacks. But I did come to understand and appreciate another common defense raised within the process: it was society's fault. And they were right. It is in many ways a double standard; students, particularly girls, are stuck between a rock and a hard place. Fashion trends dictate clothing choices in stores; which then become *must haves* for kids, who immediately swoop them in their effort to remain trendy and assimilate. And so, a double-edged sword soon appears: wear the clothes and risk being sent home from school, or don't wear the clothes and risk losing social status because the clothes are no longer cool enough.

Boys on the other hand, have fashion trends that are more commonly interchangeable from school to home, or from detention to happy hour with a fake ID. In a generalized, gender sense, the concept of dress code is inequitable. While less common, boys, too, are subject to the ramifications of their dress as they rock a brightly colored marijuana backpack to homeroom. But it's important to remember the assumptions or connotations that often are paired with such garb. Or, they think it's totally normal that their older brother (the college-aged fraternity brother) bought them that beer t-shirt with a half-naked woman on it. But again, try to remember that it's not cohesive with the learning environment of AP Chemistry. There exists a realm of dress code that impacts boys, but it is far less visible or enforced.

The parental dress code dilemma: Dress code sets into motion an unexpected dilemma for parents. Parents may want their teen to be happy, have friends, and be popular; and in their perspective, that requires some fundamental fashion standards. Teens today, living under the heavy weight of social media norms, feel expected (even by their social-hierarchy-knowing parents) to wear certain kinds of clothes to fit in. But what happens when those fashion standards are inappropriate, or objectifying, or interfere with the learning environment as defined by the school? Another parent may not really want their teen to wear a vape company t-shirt to school; but they're torn because last year was a hard year socially, and they are finally fitting in and making friends—that's what the new friends wear, and the teen wants to keep those new friends.

What's a parent to do? This is where I circle back to the importance of having a clearly defined family value system. What do you want your teenager to be known for? Appreciated for? And I ask those questions from an *at-first-glance* perspective.

Freedom of expression within an academic setting: In many ways, letting your teenager be expressive with their dress at school can be both a blessing and a curse. In an academic setting, I believe strongly that it's perfectly reasonable to restrict certain expressive parameters to maximize the learning. Yes, it is restrictive, but it also teaches a valid lesson: in life there are times and places when you don't get to make all the rules. While you may not agree with the fine print of the school dress code or you're not entirely sure an outfit your child wants to wear truly violates it, attempt to zoom out and look at the situation from a greater distance. It's the spirit of the law, not the letter of the law. For example, a workplace will have certain dress code expectations; school will not be the only time your teenager will be asked to temper their wardrobe. Fighting school dress codes is not always the best choice or the greatest learning experience for the child.

Frustrated Parent: *Where would I get shorts that are thaaaat long?* (*makes irrelevant gesture with hands)
Me: *(*thinking …)*
Frustrated Parent: *Walmart?*
Me: *(*slightly more awkward silence)*

But what happens when that over-defended teenager becomes an overly-defended-adult who wants a job? Due to their parent's dive-bomb rescue and diatribe of excuses, they effectively missed the opportunity to learn about the nuance of situational awareness. In simple terms: sometimes you just must dress a certain way—or not access the resources or opportunities within that environment.

Unimpressed, busy supervisor: *You know, you really can't wear that outfit to work.*

Overly defended teenager-turned-summer-intern: *This? I mean, c'mon it's super cute, and cost like $150 at H&M.*

Unimpressed, busy supervisor: *If you want to work here, you must comply with our dress code; we sell insurance.*

Intern: *You're objectifying me and stunting my freedom of expression.*

Supervisor: *You're going to have to go home and change.*

Intern: *I'm texting my parents.*

Supervisor: *Have them pick you up, and don't come back.*

I appreciate that parents want their child to be popular and have friends, but not at the expense of what an entitled attitude might cost them down the line. I urge parents to use the school dress code as an opportunity, as a platform to discuss where and why standards change based on setting: although we all have inherent freedoms, sometimes it's about picking what hill you want to die on.

PART 3

School & Academics

The unexpected B (or lower) grade.

So, your teen ended last semester with a B. Yes, a B, despite repeated assurances it would be an A. They had continually cited missing work, extra credit, and the final exam score as tokens of inevitable means to make the needle move back to A-land. Nonetheless, they ended with a B.

B, in this case, is for bubble. There is nothing wrong with earning a B, *if* that B is an accurate reflection of ability and effort. This section confronts a B stemming from subpar effort and study habits that are clearly below a student's known capabilities.

Bubble grades occupy real estate in two separate, but neighboring, academic GPA zip codes. Neighbors yes, but each with their own unique onramp to post-secondary educational choices. The big reveal was tense, rendered days after final exams had ended. And like a rose ceremony on a reality dating show, as the ceremony of academia unfolds, the results make more sense as the semester is reviewed and combed over in reflective detail.

Try these steps to improve your teen's academic results

★ **Learn from, don't dwell on, the grade:** Parents in this situation can frame this scenario as a blessing or a curse; I suggest the first option. Use the grade as the invitation it is to get reac-

in the protocol and process pertaining to your teen's ⌐. Use it as a wake-up call and rein in an overzealous social schedule, or calibrate organizationally ignorant patterns of behavior. Itemize, categorize, and prioritize actors that led to the bubble grade and create an action plan.

★ **Implement tangible and actionable goals:** Rather than concentrating on the obvious goal of getting an A, instead look towards smaller actions that will lead to success. Establish the expectation that your student will meet with (if only for five minutes) each teacher weekly to ensure they remain on the same page. Many schools have intervention times or teacher office hours built right into their school day. Require that your student email their teachers to schedule appointments, ask clarifying questions, or articulate their specific concerns. In time, your teen will develop self-advocacy skills that will pay dividends moving forward and into college.

★ **Establish (and stick to) a routine:** Teens thrive in structure. Implement clear procedures at home; this will help reduce stress, meltdowns, and all-nighters. Some kids use lists, some use planners, some use nothing, but most use a combination of all three. Get organized and focused by introducing a mandatory study hall of sorts. Conduct it in the same place, for the same length of time, daily, regardless of whether they have an assignment due the next day. Here, they will organize their life, calendar events, complete long-term assignments, draft correspondence, and remain in touch with their various responsibilities. Remember, you're not reading this article because last semester went according to (their) plan. Structure should also consider meal time, bed time, technology-free time, and family time as key factors in strengthening the overall wellness of your teen.

★ **Require student-teacher facetime (over or in addition to student-tutor facetime):** This is not a dig at tutors. Tutors can hold a valuable role within the educational support system for students. However, teachers are the professionals tasked with planning, teaching, and grading units of study. Facetime with teachers indicates (both verbally and nonverbally) the student's commitment to their own learning. And while final grades may not be rounded, as proven by the bubble grade, teacher-student relationships are built on countless subjective interactions that ultimately lead to a student's opportunity (or lack thereof) to complete missing work, or test corrections, or rewrite an essay and so on. The more time spent as an invested learner, the more likely students are to earn opportunities not otherwise advertised.

★ **Avoid the blame game:** Identifying factors that contributed to a lackluster final outcome is important, but overemphasizing who is the most at fault is a waste of time and energy. Many students will attribute the bubble grade to their teacher. And if asked, the teacher would most likely attribute it to the student. There is no winner. Rather, working from a collaborative mind frame will lead to more lasting and improved results. Even if you, as the parent, know 110% that it was someone's fault, lead by example and work to coalesce your student and their teacher so they can move on into the next semester with a clean slate. Teachers are professionals, but they are also people, and people are less likely to want to help someone who they perceive to be gunning for them.

Finding Academic Balance

I'm a sucker to inspirational memes. Lately, I've taken to posting them on social media. Two years ago, while working as a school administrator, writer, speaker, and advocate, I reached a tipping point. I was buried under so many responsibilities that I wasn't performing them to my full capacity. I was overcommitted and out of balance. Like any responsible adult, I complained about it to a friend.

After listening patiently, my friend replied, "It's time to take some of your own advice."

"Huh?"

"Your post, you need to follow it."

"Which one?" (Like I said, so many.)

"You can do *anything,* but not *everything.*"

Message received. It was time to create more balance in my life.

The same premise is true with teenagers. Teens are capable beings who can accomplish most academic feats with the right combination of effort and focus. But their academic eyes are often bigger than their stomachs. So, as students begin the registration process for next year's courses, it's vital to approach it with the mantra *they can do anything, but not everything.*

Consider these tips to make your child less busy, and more successful

★ **Have a plan:** A common trap when selecting courses is making hasty choices rather than slowing down to look from 30,000 feet. Effective academic planning consists of big picture thinking; it outlines all course progression scenarios (think dominos). Specific courses open certain doors in the future that others cannot. For example, challenging courses generally lead to more, while less rigorous classes lead to less. Plans are fluid, but mandatory to full understanding of how today's choices impact tomorrow's opportunities.

★ **Play to your child's strengths:** Students typically have specific subject areas that complement their natural interests and abilities. A student may prefer math and science courses over English and history courses, or vice versa. When students select honors or AP level courses in one area, they may scale back in another to increase the likelihood of success in those courses. Not to say that students shouldn't extend their academic comfort zones, but taking difficult courses void of passion and simply to line-item a resume is risky. Yes, AP level courses are important for college admissions, but taking too many or not doing well in ones taken ultimately damage the applicant's overall academic package.

★ **Factor extracurriculars into the equation:** Students are knee-deep in sports, theater, dance, leadership groups, church and community service; it is crucial to acknowledge these obligations when building an academic schedule. It's delicate: do too much and risk not keeping up, but do too little and run the risk of becoming pigeon-holed as a one-trick pony. Finding and remaining committed to a few meaningful activities far outweighs a frenetic spattering of activities over the course of high school. That said, these activities take time and cannot thrive under the weight of an unrealistic academic burden. Again, balance.

★ **Fight the urge to comply with others' expectations:** Your child is your child; they may or may not be blessed with the same academic, athletic, or artistic DNA as your neighbor's child. Knowing what your friends' kids are taking is a dangerous game. I get it, you want to scope out the competition. There are two flaws with this strategy: viewing the admissions process as a competition, and mistaking their child's path for your child's path. Your child should only be competing against the contrast between their potential and their results. Results from previous courses paired with college goals should dictate next year's classes, not what you've heard others are taking. Your child is unique; if you attempt to cram them into the box of another student's pedigree you will trigger revolt, apathy, or unhappiness.

★ **Focus on the whole child:** Many times, it is the child who requests the overly demanding schedule. If that's the case, utilize a school counselor to talk through the cost-benefits of the proposed schedule. What is the upside? Drawbacks? If determined to be best for the child, look for other places to lower obligations to balance the demand stemming from this rigorous course load. Ultimately parents may need to exercise the power of veto to keep balance for their child.

★ **Moving forward:** Remember, students can do anything, but not everything, and something's gotta give. If you don't identify that give now, the give will show up unannounced to wreak havoc. So, in planning, view your options through the lens of *balance*.

Parenting in the World of Academics

In this activity we will examine your approach to handling and addressing high school academics. We will examine your child's strengths, weaknesses, their motivators, and your overall management. This section will help you understand the difference between process and product within the context of education.

Directions: Notate which you would consider a strength of your teenager. Any items left unchecked will be considered a liability.

○ Reading comprehension   ○ Self-advocacy

○ Writing   ○ Buy-in

○ Math   ○ Teacher relationships

○ Science   ○ Teacher communication

○ Social Studies/History   ○ Test preparation

○ Organization   ○ Test-taking skills

○ Study habits

Reflect: Which of the educational elements is their greatest strength? Which is their greatest weakness?

Second Look: Place a star next to any weakness that is not being currently or effectively addressed. Use this to drive your parenting plan and next steps.

Tipping Point

Directions: Identify which academic triggers mobilize action within your parenting. What gets you fired up?

○ Missing assignments   ○ Lack of routine

○ Low scores on tests and quizzes   ○ Formal report card

○ Tardy to or missing classes   ○ Late assignments

○ Snapshot look at grades (usually online)   ○ Being unorganized

Motivators

Directions: Identify the tools you use as motivators to prevent or ways to react to poor academic performance.

○ Curfew

○ Grounding

○ Increased chores

○ Taking away technology

○ Limiting access to friends

○ Cancelling social media

○ Driving/ridesharing

○ Allowance

An Exercise in Your Focus

Directions: In the grid below list your student's current or most recent class schedule, teacher and letter grade.

Course	Teacher	Letter Grade

Reflection: Did you find you were more aware of their grades than any other aspect? Do you know their teachers' names?

Interventions Query

Directions: Identify the interventions and strategies you employ when supporting academic progress. Make notes next to the list with examples.

○ Find subject-specific tutors

○ Define study time

○ Define study location

○ Require teacher communication

○ Assist with organization

○ Expect use of school interventio

○ Assist with time management

○ Expect a calendar is kept

○ Enforce a regular eat/sleep rout

○ Limit social activities to avoid burnout

Reflection:

★ What (if anything) do you not utilize currently but will now consider doing?

★ Which intervention on the list do you rely on the most? Your crutch?

★ What parenting habit are you willing to alter to look for new results?

Tip: Focus on interventions that skill-build and encourage and increase accountability. Calendaring and scheduling appointments for your student is perhaps time-saving and an action you've always taken, but amounts to passing the baton; drawing your teen into performing that process (rather than waiting for you to do it) will increase their buy-in and accountability in the change process. A student who is scheduling a tutor for themselves, after acknowledging that they need extra support, will be far more tutor-able than the one who has his mother forcing him to an appointment he didn't knew he had and doesn't think he needs. Obviously, there is a way to lead your student to the conclusion that they need extra help, even those who have been previously reluctant to admit it, but that typically only occurs when promoted to a co-decision maker in the family decision-making process.

Product vs. Process

Product	Process
Report Cards	Study Routines and Habits
GPA	Involvement at School
Test Scores	Organization and Planning
Detentions	Tardiness and Absences

Clarification of Concept: Process is defined by the small steps between the mile markers of product. By focusing on process, the product takes care of itself. Product is still important, but by overemphasizing the final outcomes found in product, you risk ignoring the critical lifelong skills found in process.

Process = Structure: Teenagers thrive in structure. They do well when they know precisely what is expected of them and what will happen when they do not take care of business.

Process is:

✓ What they do

✓ How they do it

✓ Where they do it

✓ When they do it

✓ Why they do it

✓ What happens when they do

✓ What happens when they don't

Product = results: Teenagers earn the product because of the process. Dedication to the process heightens their likelihood to capture, claim, and collect product. Product is capital.

Product is:

✓ Report cards

✓ Test scores

✓ Quiz scores

✓ College admissions

✓ Scholarships

✓ Awards

✓ Job opportunities

Reality: when complaining about a teacher, teenagers typically refer to a few staple descriptors:

- Teacher is not organized
- Teacher is inconsistent in reactions to student choices and behavior
- Teacher lacks control of the classroom
- Teacher is gone a lot
- Teacher doesn't actively engage or teach or seem invested in students
- The class has no sense of routine (don't know what to expect)

Irony: Many of those same descriptors also relate to teenagers' primary complaints about their parents and household:

- They (themselves) are unorganized
- Parents are inconsistent in their reactions to their choices and behavior
- Parents don't assert control of their comings and goings
- Teen and parents are like ships passing in the night
- Parents aren't properly or actively engaged with overall being and wellness
- Teen lacks routine (study, eat, tutor, sports, rest, friends, family)

Creating structure for your teenager: It is imperative that you create and maintain a structured environment from which to operate and reach maximum capacity. Structure is proactive, a departure from the reactive tools parents commonly utilize (such as tutors).

If you build the fence, they'll play in the yard: Establish protocol for expected behaviors and routines from your teenagers. Once those expectations are built, visible and interconnected, they allow the teenager to operate without a layer of excuse-creating ambiguity. *Example: They will study for 60 minutes each evening at the kitchen table, no exceptions.*

Tips for creating academic structure

★ **Create a neutral study command center:** I strongly recommend having your teens complete their daily allotted study time in a neutral space. It cannot be their own room; in addition to the inherent distractions in a teenager's room, the possessive nature of the space makes it hard for you to check in on them without barging into their room, or asking them to turn down their music, or unlock the door. The neutral space is a kitchen table, home office, or any table free from distraction and within view. The neutral space is a bit uncomfortable (in a preferential sense) for the teen, which will motivate them to get it done and over with.

★ **Maintain forward thinking:** A vital component of this structure is placing the accountability on the student. With them (not *for* them) sit down and outline and mark critical dates. Example: end of a quarter, end of semester, dates of final exams, any and all available dates for large assignments, quizzes, projects, and exams. This creates a natural roadmap for them to follow ... specifically when you ask them what they are working on and they quip, "I don't have any home-work."

★ **Utilize backwards planning:** Once the key dates are established, a study and completion plan for each event is notated on the calendar, with their efforts amortized over time, rather than cramming with a tutor for five hours two days before an exam. More work over time will result in less reactionary and emotional outcomes.

★ **Embrace an accountability calendar:** Employees are accountable to their employers, and your children, in a sense, are your employees. Each day that they work within the clearly defined and expected time and space, they need to record what they accomplish. This is not merely writing "math"; rather, they would write "math: page 145 odd." This lets you know (when you need to) what they have been up to. If the final product does not match their alleged calendar, you know it's time to tighten your level of oversight; when they do match, you know it's okay to lay off a bit.

★ **Proactive habits decrease reactive responses:** By following the above steps you will discover that far fewer reactionary events occur: less emergency tutors, less teen-parent conflict, fewer motivators (as listed earlier) needed, and will notice far more autonomy, ownership, and confidence in managing the many academic tasks they have ahead of them.

Key takeaways:

✓ Build a fence (process requirements)

✓ Neutral space (study command center)

✓ Forward thinking (key dates and due dates)

✓ Backwards planning (efforts over time)

✓ Accountability (record work done each day)

Next steps: Which of these elements do you already have in place? What steps do you need to take to build your fence?

Teacher communication protocol: Teachers can be the biggest ally in a student's success and ability to put the wheels back on the academic wagon. Too often, teachers are positioned as the antagonist and the student as the victim. Having been in formal education for 14 years I can tell you this is not typically true. Sure, some teachers are total cranks and seemingly feed off punishing or restricting student performance. But most are not. Teachers want their students to be successful, but they also need to know that the student is an engaged member of the change process. Teacher communication is a valuable skill and cannot be understated in its importance.

Tips for student-teacher communication

★ **Get to know teachers:** Establish a relationship base early and maintain that relationship throughout the year so that the teacher is not approached only in times of need or crisis. Teachers are humans, people, too—encourage your student to find connection points: sports, politics, travel, TV shows, hobbies, family. Whatever the case, the footing is important equity in the relationship bank.

★ **Avoid the ambush:** Confronting or approaching a teacher about a mistake, error, questionable grade or similar is best done without a peer audience. Encourage your student to make an appointment via email (or in person first, but memorialized in email) to find a time that the teacher will be present and prepared to discuss the need.

★ **Email, email, email:** Many teachers use email and prefer it to drive-by student questions and comments due to the sheer volume of information they are responsible for remembering and responding to. Email serves two fundamental purposes: it allows you to get your thoughts together in a cohesive and unemotional tone, and tracks the student's attempt to resolve the issue, need, query, or whatever the case, so that later in the game they cannot and will not be accused of not making their best effort. I hear often, and saw this frequently as a high school administrator, that teachers tell students NOT to email them and they WON'T respond to email. Perfect. Email anyway. Email your confirmations of verbally scheduled appointments, verbally agreed-upon grade resolutions and anything else that could eventually become an I-said-Teacher-said situation.

★ **Be specific, and prepared:** When seeking extra attention or assistance from teachers, it is most effective to be specific and prepared with those specific questions for your time together. Most likely, the teacher will be aiding other students as well, or has a limited amount of time for individual attention. If your student scores low on a quiz, but is working to perform better on their upcoming exam, the quiz provides them with targeted areas for help, rather than simply walking in and saying: "I don't get it!" On the writing side of the curriculum, students who are specific about what part of the writing process is troubling them will get much better use of their time if they have put in some self-assessment work prior to the meeting. For example, the student who approaches with a targeted need, such as transition sentences, or how to craft a thesis statement, will gain more benefit from the session than one who simply says: "I can't write."

★ **Practice patience:** The links in the chain reaction of unfinished business and the consequences that accompany them (think missing assignments, false zeros, waiting for late work to be graded) can cause students to go from assertive to annoying from the perspective of the teachers. Encourage your student to allow time for items to be resolved and pay mind to the cause for the delay. For example, if your student turned in an essay late because they were ill, say a week late, then they should expect their work to be reciprocally late in its return. Generally, a good rule of thumb is a two-week turnaround time on work to be graded (except for formal essays—those take much longer to grade). If your student has been patiently waiting and there is not a resolution, they should … you guessed it! Email! It's a receipt documenting their effort to resolve the problem.

Teaching teens to email: Have you ever watched a teen construct an email? It's painful. Lowercase letters dominate would-be capitalization; words like "you" get all texty and slide in as u; they're void of formal greetings and salutations. I could go on. That said, it's not their fault.

As adults, we take email for granted. It's ingrained into the fiber of our daily and expected communication process. Yet, despite its value, email is one of the most under-emphasized skills taught today. Email is critical for your teenager throughout high school, during the college admissions process, in college and on into their job hunt, and still, we barely show them how to do it.

Creating a mature email address: Every teen needs a respectable and identifiable email account. Yes, in third grade surfer135@ whatever.com was cute, but as a teenager communicating with teachers, potential employers, or admissions officials, it screams immaturity. Avoid sophomoric monikers at all costs. So now they have email. Check. But just because they have it, doesn't mean they'll use it. A mother recently told a story of her son who went weeks without knowing he was admitted to his dream school because they notified him via email. Thus, part of the training process is establishing the routine of checking it. Regularly.

Teen hesitation: A typical teen approaches email with a *what's the point* mind frame. Why? It's slow and outdated, in the same way my generation views *snail mail*. They don't use it frequently, if at all, and when tasked with sending an email, upon the realization that there are no emojis, they can't even function. And so, a really poorly constructed email is born.

The value in school: On the school front, email is vital when documenting and clarifying a teen's educational needs. As the teens draft their first few emails, parents should review them to ensure the message is communicated clearly. Obviously, no parent should be drafting emails for their teen, nor reviewing them in the long term, but as the skill is crafted, oversight and feedback have lasting positive results.

As I teacher, I loved emails from students. Really? Yes. Most of my inbox was dominated by peers or parents. So students who could communicate clearly and succinctly were a breath of fresh air for an overworked and inundated teacher. When students emailed me, it provided me with valuable feedback and insight.

In times of conflict or misunderstanding, a well-worded email from a student effectively front-loads and disarms the teacher. This is a welcome reprieve from the drive-by approach from a nervous or emotional student during passing period or class, both of which can often be perceived as an ambush or inappropriate. Emails to teachers typically result in invitations to meet. A scheduled appointment reduces anxiety as the student feels expected and welcome. Once together, and based on the email, the content of the student-teacher meeting is more efficient and productive.

This leads to the obvious counterpunch of what happens when the teacher won't or doesn't respond. Email is great in that all emails are time-stamped and clear evidence that the student is trying to resolve the issue at hand. No, you can't guarantee the teacher's actions, but a student can position themselves advantageously by polite, meaningful and regular emails on the matter at hand. Even unanswered emails can prevent the *too little too late* scenarios that non-communicative students face. It's one thing when students make no attempt to resolve issues prior to report cards, and quite another when they do.

Transferrable skill: There is the transference of this skill to other aspects of a teen's future life. During the college admissions process, the concept of expressed interest is becoming increasingly meaningful to admissions officials. In short, it's how many times the applicant made contact beyond simply applying. Correspondence is a large piece of this concept, and email is the bread and butter.

A comment from a college senior on my article from last week read, "... emails between yourself and the professor are the most important factors in college. They are crucial. Learning to utilize these skills in high school will be incredibly beneficial for your college career, rather than having to learn them once you're there." Straight from the horse's mouth. Communication skills, including email, are undeniably valuable in the success of your teen, future college student, and gainfully employed young adult.

Building academic autonomy in your teen: A picture that went viral last year was of a simple sign taped to the door of a school in Arkansas. It reads, *"Stop! If you are dropping off your son's forgotten lunch, books, homework, equipment etc., please TURN AROUND and exit the building. Your son will learn to problem-solve in your absence."* While extremely blunt, the sign accurately summarizes a growing frustration in education: the saturation of overly-involved high school parents. These parents regularly meddle in, fix, engineer, and master-mind their teens' daily lives. They intercept teachable moments from the hands of their children, thereby preventing the acquisition of a much-needed life skill: autonomy.

Developing autonomy is like riding a bike: difficult to master, but impossible to forget. Even as years pass between bike rides, the brain easily recalls how to proceed. The same holds true with autonomy; developed early, it can be effectively utilized in adulthood. But just like riding a bike, it takes practice. High school is crucial in the process of life skill development; it's an opportunity for teens to experience grit-producing scenarios. When denied such formative experiences, life's future challenges are forever exacerbated by its absence.

Try these five practices as your teen navigates middle and high school

★ **Don't address issues with teachers before your teenager does:**
The two people best fit to resolve a classroom conflict are

the student and teacher. Swooping in prematurely will cause defensive posturing from the teacher and complicate the resolution process. Parents can instead redirect this energy and teach their teen how to think through, organize, and properly record their thoughts in an email to their teacher. Not only will this memorialize communication, it also provides insight into the student-teacher interactions from a healthy distance. Teens need effective communication skills, and parents can teach, but not supplant those skills.

★ **Let go of your fear of teacher retaliation against your teenager:** Teacher retaliation is never accepted, and is certainly addressed when it occurs (though instances are rare). Still, parents avoid teacher contact in fear of retaliation against their child. However, teachers typically already know the source of complaints; they are anticipated, and warnings to superiors are issued. When parents attempt to avoid teachers, it actually causes more harm than good; it makes the conflict become adult versus adult, taking focus away from the true focal point: the student. Circumventing teachers denies teenagers an opportunity to practice resiliency skills. Tense conversations function similarly to training wheels on a bike. Teens need to hear feedback from their teacher, and teachers from their students; even if that only means agreeing to disagree, it's important that each is given an opportunity to be heard. More often than not, both student and teacher walk away with a better understanding and heightened level of respect for one another. However, if a student feels they are being subjected to retaliation, it should be immediately reported to administration; for it is only when behaviors are exposed, that behaviors change.

★ **When your teen gets home from school, don't talk to them about school:** Reflect on the end of a long work day; there's an element of decompression required to transition from work to home. The same is true with teens; they need time to decompress when they arrive home. Although they're thinking about school, they aren't ready to discuss it. Teens require the mental real estate to operate without immediately being asked to rehash school with their parents. Without a school-free buffer, teens will avoid talking to parents at all costs. Once the norm of school-free discussions is established, teens can become more willing to communicate, which in turn, provides a natural transition into school-related topics.

★ **Ignore the manifestations and look for underlying issues:** School performance is a portal into the teen psyche; it has little to do with school, and really is a reflection of their mental and emotional state. Parents mistakenly focus too much on specific grades rather than trigger points. Parents can instead attempt to ignore the small stuff, and subtly look for deeper issues causing the manifestation. Teens will only engage with parents for so long, so don't waste it nitpicking. With enough patience, parents can find an approach that yields enough honesty to eventually reveal the root cause. Until a cause is identified, there can be no solution.

★ **Help your teenager develop lifelong skills:** Can you imagine if every time a teenager wanted to ride a bike, the teen still required a parent to run alongside as they attempted to peddle?! So why do parents still embrace this practice with school? The bike-riding children were initially appropriately supported and protected (think helmet, training wheels, hands-on assistance). But gradually, these were scaled back until no longer needed. The child was supplied with the tools, time, and training to be independently successful. The same approach can be used in helping teenagers hone resiliency skills. The role of parent is to help their teen to become independent and capable. Instead of emailing a teacher, parents can help their teen articulate thoughts; instead of rushing to administration, parents can prepare their teenager to speak directly with the teacher; instead of nitpicking assessment scores, parents can create dialogue that will reveal root causes of mediocre performance. In so doing, parents can take their hands off the bike and watch their child ride successfully, and resiliently, off to college.

Although I strongly advocate for your teen to handle their lower level roadblocks free from parent engagement, here are some suggestions to maximize the effectiveness of your presence and involvement when it does occur:

★ **Understanding the school food chain:** At times, as a parent, you will find yourself rightfully angry with a grading or discipline decision rendered by the school. Many parents try to zip their way all the way to the top, only to be returned to the beginning. Like Monopoly, you must pass Go, and follow required motions to get to your destination (which very well could be the top-level school district personnel). Most schools have a student handbook that outlines the formal complaint, grievance, and communication procedures—but here are some generally accepted communication funnels.

Example of school district hierarchy:
- Teacher
- Department Chair (teacher heading the curricular department)
- Guidance Counselor
- Assistant Principal/Dean
- Principal
- Director of X (X = District department that has jurisdiction)
    Example: Director of Curriculum and Instruction = grades; Director of Student Services = discipline; Director of Special Education = IEP/504
- Assistant Superintendent
- Superintendent
- School Board

Parent-school communication tips

★ **Stay optimistic:** Despite your best efforts, it's tempting to get and stay negative. Negative posturing with teachers, counselors, and school officials stagnates the process and injects emotions into an already complicated teenager-heavy world. Do your best to enter the situation with a belief that a solution is possible, and be willing to compromise along the way.

★ **Check your tone:** Email has become the primary mode of communication for busy school professionals. Tone in email is very hard to discern and defensive teachers tend to interpret parent messages with a defensive posture. Be careful to read your emails and screen for statements that can be misconstrued. Again, if your end-game involves a resolution that you will like and benefit your student, all parts of the process matter. And besides, being polite and gracious is better than being a mean-emailing parent.

★ **Respect the hierarchy:** No, you can't go straight to the top. And while some parents email school board presidents or the superintendent—they ultimately end up back at the beginning of the process, going through the motions, but having offended the very people they need to meet with in the process. You will get to the top of the hierarchy if you want or need to, but patience and following the process is part of the process.

★ **Make appointments:** Nobody likes a drive-by parent who swoops in and unloads with an unorganized and rushed delivery. On the off-chance you do get seen without an appointment, chances are you will have a short window to deliver your message, perhaps not enough time to correctly outline your case or situation, and end up seeming unorganized and frantic. After the drive-by, when you do get an appointment, it will be put to the back of the line as they won't want to see you again right away (or at all) based on your first frenetic interaction. So, make an appointment—it will make you look better and allow time for all parties to be more prepared for, and productive in, the meeting itself.

★ **Be direct, but respectful:** Being direct is commendable: say what you came to say, but avoid overly-antagonistic statements. Even if you have a totally warranted claim to introduce (let's say against a teacher who is 100% at fault) do so in a manner that leaves you aboveboard. Once you say something that is a low-blow or mean (and irrelevant) the meeting becomes about you and what you said, not about the issue at hand. Say what you need to say, but mind your manners—that is, if you truly want a resolution that favors your student.

★ **Hold your teenager accountable:** In any meeting, about anything, you will most likely encounter a rebuttal of some sort, and that will almost certainly entail a less than appealing fact about your child. Blindly defending your child and dismissing any negative feedback as baseless will serve you little in a school meeting. Be willing and able to listen to feedback and accept that your student has some skin in the game. Parents who can accept accountability for their child receive markedly different decisions and responses than those who are seemingly unwilling or unable to fathom that their child is anything less than a perfect human. Kids are humans, yes, but mistakes are their pastime—it's okay.

★ **Consider your threats:** Hurling threats, specifically legal threats, in a meeting is a wonderful way to end a meeting. There's nothing wrong with seeking legal representation when warranted, but that representation needs to be introduced thoughtfully and minus the pomp and circumstance. School districts are used to litigation and equipped with legal reps either in-house or out-sourced. When you bring an attorney unannounced, the meeting will end immediately. Legal representation has its place in the edu-landscape, but it slows down the process tremendously and injects levels of scrutiny that handcuff a principal's ability to communicate freely and openly with you. So, pick your battles.

Combatting downward trends in your student's academics: Resilience is not something you can order off Etsy or Amazon Prime; it is old-fashioned; it doesn't accept credit cards and must be earned in an *uphill both ways in the snow* sort of way. Resilience is not something parents can command children to absorb and utilize; it is a quality, however, that parents must themselves embrace and demonstrate when children exhibit long stretches of uninspiring, unattractive, and historically uncharacteristic behaviors.

Here are the common phases parents pass through when their child is declining rapidly in their academic performance:

★ **Phase One: spending too much time looking backwards:**
Broken-hearted parents often find themselves in the office of a school administrator, counselor, psychologist, or spin class. Venting. Searching. Problem-solving. Crying. Struggling. They arrive inexplicably stuck in the void between unconditional love and pure frustration; between excuses and blame; but mostly, willing to do anything in their power to fix it. But they get tripped up by uncertainty as to exactly how.

These meetings typically begin in tones reminiscent of an easier time. Folders spill out old awards, certificates, and report cards from elementary school. *She was one of the smartest students in her third-grade class, even the lead in her play, and now ... she is barely surviving, let alone thriving.* Parents are yearning to recapture that magic recipe that produced happiness, innate curiosity, and success-come-early-and-often. This initial grieving phase is very emotional and somewhat protracted, but a necessary step to moving toward establishing a lasting resolution. I reference the phase as *necessary,* but I *do not* recommend wallowing in it for too long.

★ **Phase Two: overreacting and doing everything at once:**
Parents rightfully look for a quick fix to return their child to the happy, curious, high-performer that once dominated the carpool and kitchen table with laughter and tales of accomplishments. It's normal; for example, when my daughter has a fever I grab Motrin. After a certain point, there is only so much Motrin one can have before either a) the fever breaks or b) you head to the doctor. Unwittingly, many families mis-

takenly embrace a Motrin management plan as opposed to searching for a true diagnosis. They just give Motrin (so to speak) repeatedly. This is largely due to the mirage-like positives that initially stem from such triage. Grades temporarily rise, behaviors quickly calm with certain restrictions ... and order is superficially restored. Understandably, this approach bears quick results in this busy life we lead, but does not treat the actual root cause of the child's symptoms. While such techniques like taking a phone or car away are useful, they are ineffective in times of significant adversity and stress. Parents can easily get stuck on this hamster wheel; treating a cut with band-aids when it actually needs stitches.

Alternately, some families go overboard and implement a new and overly rigid infrastructure that does indeed produce results when assembled and monitored, but otherwise proves fruitless when the child is returned to their true environment. Vital to this process is the search for longevity in a potential resolution, and not the speed with which a resolution is reached. Quick is not better; real is better.

★ **Phase Three: rallying others to help "get" your teenager:**
Understanding and evaluating your child to determine if the plateau is hormonal, cognitive, substance induced, emotional, situational, or a combination therein is key when creating a family plan to address your concerns. Teens will eventually (typically) hit their individual threshold or plateau of intellectual curiosity; subsequently, without a defined passion or point of optimism, their typical behavior and academic performance will decrease, sometimes at alarming rates. Teens also shift their curiosity and reprioritize from traditional to edgy. In this phase parents should strategically and patiently dig for the root cause of the outward symptoms manifested through negative behaviors and low academic outcomes. Knowing the true cause will be the only way to reach the longevity of a real remedy. Anything short of that is, well ... Motrin.

So how do I do this? Imagine you are having Thanksgiving dinner, and you are going to invite every influential adult in your child's life, *and perhaps one mental health professional.* I repeat, their life, not yours. Think. Who are they? Where do they sit at the table? Why are they influential? Start here. This is your list. They can begin to turn the ship.

These influencers hold the ticket into the mind of your child. They know your child in a way others do not; this knowledge when combined with their relationship can get them access through a door, that to you as a parent has been closed (and most likely slammed) in your face. They also don't know what they don't know; they aren't so subjectively or emotionally close to the fire. That distance makes their paradigm uniquely different from your own. Rely on them; allow them to help you help your child. Give control away to get control back.

Imagine these influencers taking your child to breakfast or coffee, or to a baseball game, or surfing, or shooting baskets ... and in that process, they begin to thaw the iceberg; each conversation shaves a piece of ice away until at last, the real issue is exposed. Be careful what you wish for; you cannot unknow what you will learn; but you can't live as a prisoner of their angst either.

Tips for parents when dealing with a child's declining grades and performance

★ **It's okay to reflect on the past, but live in the present:** What your children did in 5th grade means little when they are a junior in high school. The immense physical, emotional, and cognitive changes that teenagers experience from middle school through high school is wicked, and entirely unpredictable. Reflecting on the past is mildly productive when done correctly. Boosting a teen's ego, or attempting to rebuild their confidence by bringing up projects or assignments from years ago stem from old thinking that's obsessed with product. I bet you remember the grade they earned, the score. That's great, but it's not now, here in this present moment of their struggling life. Is there anything now, regardless of how teeny-tiny it seems, which they are doing well? Not grades! That's product. We're focusing on a shifted emphasis on process. Maybe they are on time every day? Or give 100% every time they step foot on the lacrosse field?

★ **Embrace shoulder time:** By the time you arrive to a place that warrants a conversation regarding their academic vibrancy, I imagine there is a lot you want to say and address. Check yourself before you wreck yourself. Too much too soon will kill the conversation. The goal here is dialogue and not a parent monologue. Sitting down at the kitchen table is also an effective way to suck the productive air out of the room. Instead, use shoulder time. As the name suggests, it's carved out of time spent next to your child. Think chair-lift skiing, at a baseball game, on a road trip (only if they're riding shotgun), at a loud and large restaurant dinner. Pick a time when their guard is down, and you can simply pick their brain to get some form of self-reflection or self-assessment. Please do not confuse this with an ambush. It is not the time to list all the ways they are dissimilar to their 10-year-old self. This is, however, an excellent time to ask some open-ended questions. For example: what class do you feel most successful in right now? Why? What makes it different from a class you're feeling unsuccessful in right now? Oh, really, what's that class? Where are you feeling frustrated with that class? What can I do to help you? And so on. Gentle. Subtle. And then zip it. You get a maximum of eight minutes.

★ **Engage influencers and positive role models:** You'll find I mention this a few times in this book, and that's because teens respond better to third party influencers. Sometimes doing your homework doesn't seem so damn annoying if you get to do it with your uncle at Starbucks while he works remotely. Sometimes you cannot, for whatever reason, articulate your hopes and dreams, or regrets and fears, to your mom or dad, but can easily reveal them to your little league coach-turned neighbor. If you feel stuck, or ignored, turn to another trusted adult to deliver your message and retrieve your information.

★ **Change the routine:** Nothing changes if nothing changes. Sometimes raising teens calls for a batch of shock and awe. We'll address this in more detail later, but teens are creatures of habits and operate in strict habit loops, their standard operating procedure: where they study, when, how long, with whom, distractions, how or if they seek extra teacher support, their level of communication, etc. Breaking their ineffective habits sometimes needs to be part of a habit-loop disruption, whereby their overall routine is disrupted, deconstructed, and rebuilt. You already do this when you ground them, or take a phone, or keys to the car.

Examples of changes in routine:

✓ Earlier bed time

✓ Earlier wake-up time

✓ Location where they study

✓ Proximity to technology and other distractions

✓ Ability to participate in extracurricular activities

✓ Access to social events and friends

Considering a school move: When a teenager is in the room with you, whether it be at the doctor, tutor, psychologist, or wherever, include them in the conversation. I know this sounds simple. But it's one of the most common mistakes I see adults make. Too often parents will talk about their teen (*who is sitting next to them and across from me*) as if they aren't even in the room. Including teenagers in conversations and the decision-making process establishes ownership and increases the odds of a teenager's buy-in with the final outcome, even when that outcome is not what the teenager would choose for him or herself.

Okay, so I'm telling you to include them, but how? A good place to begin is by asking them the same questions you are asking yourself about the situation in question. These questions should be related to the drivers (think push and pull) of your decision. Examples of drivers are fear or hope. What are your fears within the context of your consideration, and how are they impacting your thought process? Or, what are the hopes you have thrown onto the back of this potential choice, and how are those hopes to affect your judgement?

Let's take for example, a common scenario in which a family is considering whether or not to move their struggling teenager to a new school for a fresh start. Many times, the conversations and dialogue surrounding the potential move are had and processed by all but the actual person with boots on the ground, the teen. Including them in the pros-and-cons-party, despite being more initial work that simply omitting them from it, will pay large dividends in the end. This does not mean that parents must get their teen's blessing or permission prior to making an educational change. In fact, more than not, teens cannot see what is best for them like their parents can. Or even if they know deep down that a change is needed, they cannot acuate that internal whisper into a well-articulated statement. So they end up partaking in the most cliché *cry for help* via poor grades, a sour attitude, or total isolationism. Or all three if you're lucky.

Here are some considerations for a family considering a school move:

✓ What are the academic benefits of remaining at your current school site?

✓ What are the academic advantages of moving to the proposed school?

✓ What behaviors suggest that you (your teen) are unhappy at your current school site?

✓ What advice would you give someone else in your situation about the school move?

✓ What are your biggest fears about making a school move?

✓ Can you think of any solutions, tools, or resources that will address those fears?

✓ How many of those fears are totally made up?

✓ What evidence do you have that makes you think those fears are realistic?

✓ What is the worst-case scenario of not making a school change?

Look below the surface: This type of questions help parents sort of the true underlying issue that surface as decisions like a school move. School moves have a time and place. In fact, my parents moved me after a continued downward social and academic spiral, allowing for a fresh start in seventh grade. However, what my parents missed then, and what parents miss all the time, is the opportunity to debrief and dig in, to discover what, if any, social emotional ramifications exist under the surface.

Not always the answer: As parents, we want to save our children, that is our job. And one way to save someone is to remove them from a harmful situation. However, with schools, the DNA that create vulnerable and trying times for adolescents are eerily similar from school to school. Yes, one can debate public and private, or big and small and so on. But the core social dynamics and interpersonal and emotional landmines are based mostly on the specific child himself, and how they are prepared, condition, and supported during those awkward and challenging times.

Details to consider when vetting a potential school move:

★ **Impact on GPA:** Grade weighting varies by school district. One may issue a "grade bump" for an honors course, while another may not. This means GPAs are recalculated when the student enters the new district. A student exiting a district who issues "grade bumps" may see their GPA drop based on the absence of the bump in the new district.

★ **Impact on current class schedule:** Not all high schools (even within the same district) offer the same courses. It's important to understand what classes will be available when moving. College requirements work in years, not semesters.

For example, let's say your teen is taking an AP European History course, has completed a semester, and then transfers to a school without that course offering. Your teen will need to complete the second half of that course somewhere, on their own time, to finish that full year of history to satisfy college requirements. One half of one history class, and one half of another history course, will not work.

★ **Impact on athletic participation:** Sanctioned high school athletics are monitored by third party organizations. Those organizations have rules and safeguards in place for transfers, largely to prevent students from moving solely for athletic reasons. When your student changes schools, pay attention to those rules and work within them to maintain athletic eligibility. In fact, many cap the number of transfers allowed in a high school career, and too many transfers result in a red flag, and result in ineligibility for up to one calendar year. Transferring during off-season periods has less impact than in season.

★ **Impact on family logistics:** How will the new school affect others in the family and their routines? Understanding the family dominos is vital. For example, if you are making a huge accommodation by transferring one of your children to a school that will result in every other member of the family assuming a new routine, brace for impact. Kids are creatures of habit. Frontloading others and drawing them into the conversation will pay dividends.

★ **Impact of college admissions:** High school transfers based on relocation are a non-issue. But, several high school transfers within the same zip code of geography may cause a college admission official to wonder. Frankly, many significant discipline situations result in transfers. Due to educational laws, the details or even acknowledgement of those incidents is forbidden. Thus, admissions counselors look to patterns that resemble or seem strange. One transfer within the same region is fine, and normal, but two or more may cause red flags.

If you are considering a school move, consider what is going on below the surface first. A move might be less the answer than instead confronting what you discover with the proper professional support.

A common mistake: comparing your children: In my own parenting, I frequently catch myself assessing my younger children's progress through the lens of my oldest. Do they walk when she did? Or read like she can? Or express thoughts and words or emote compassion like she does? Are they like her? And the easy to forget, yet glaringly obvious answer to this, is no. They are not her; they are their own beings, and deserve to be treated as such. But even as I consciously remind myself of this, the next week I find myself at the pediatrician, firing off some remark about how child number two hasn't done X, Y or blah, blah, blah. So, I get it, it's easy to say that you parent your child uniquely as their own being, but more difficult to do.

I coach parents, many parents, successfully through this dilemma. Take for example, the family who books an appointment when considering potential courses for their teen to take during the following academic school year. During our meeting, there are at least three times that I will pause to gently remind the parents that the anecdotal child in their comments is not the teen in the conversation; we're trying to find classes for a younger sibling, and yet time and again, the parents circle back to the oldest. Why? The oldest child was a real go-getter who succeeded in a very linear and traditional sense: straight As, glowing remarks from teachers on report cards, ability to clearly articulate feeling,; made friends easily. And on.

"Well, my oldest took AP Biology and AP Psychology," they'll say.

Well that child also had the intrinsic motivation and innate academic skill set to take those classes. I'll think ....

"That isn't Sam, though," I'll respond. "Sam, you prefer art and seem very passionate about writing. Sam, (*looking at Sam, since he's in the room, you know)* have you considered taking Digital Photography and AP Language?"

"Digital Photography! That's a real throw-away class! No college is going to want him if he takes that class." Again, Sam's right next to her. And she's getting all *him* on him, as if he's not there. This type of subjective analysis, based purely off Sam's older sister, is not really a boost for the self-esteem, and certainly is one tone-deaf monologue from a parent failing to grasp the fact that her children, are in fact, different children.

But it also can be the other way around. Perhaps the oldest was a real screw-up; they failed most classes, were kicked out of class, and was in most ways a loner. Parents in this scenario often enable the younger child or children, and set a bar so low based on the data points of their older children, and lack confidence that each child can be uniquely successful.

Tips for having meaningful conversations regarding academic progress and endeavors.

★ **Treat your child as their own person and unique student:** Little derails a meaningful or productive conversation with a younger sibling more than an opening statement by a parent highlighting all the ways the older brother or sister outshined this child. Honestly, if there was ever a time to pretend you had no other children, it is whenever you are talking to one of the younger ones about changes you would like them to make in their academic world. Use any other example you want; any, just not the siblings. Please.

★ **Unite behind a shared point of frustration:** Your conversations will go further and be more effective if it assumes the identity of a dialogue and not a monologue. Easier said than done; many teens simply don't want to speak to their parents, and love utilizing simple statements like *I don't know* or anything equally frustrating for parents. But one saving grace about teenagers is that they are largely narcissistic. Translation: they love talking about themselves. I rarely encourage bagging on teachers or coaches, but little unites foes like a common enemy. Broach conversations with something you both agree that you disagree with, like a teacher who is particularly mean, or a coach who is unappreciative of their talent. This warms their engines, validates their thinking, and can, when done properly, open the flood gates.

★ **Include your child in emails, meetings, conversations:** By the time you have yourself a high school-aged child, gone are the days of excluding them, or shielding them from correspondence about their educational welfare. It is, after all, their life. A common trap is to insulate them (or attempt to) by circumventing them and working around them with regard to what is being said about them. Well-intentioned insulation tends to backfire in the long run. It's important for the student to be part of the conversation—to hear the feedback, even if it's uncomfortable to process at times, to resolve or confront the issue hindering their academic success. The biggest change-agent in the school equation will be your student: not their teacher, counselor, or therapist. Those stakeholders are integral in gathering data points, observations, ideas, and interventions; but it will rest squarely on the willingness and buy-in of the student to get ideas and interventions out of the idea-phase and into the action-phase. Too often a plethora of communication has taken place behind the scenes, and when presented to the student, feels more like an ambush and less like an organic conversation or plan of better habits with the goal to achieve better results in the future. If you want buy-in from your student, they must be part of the process from the beginning.

★ **Focus on targeted conversations (think laser, not shotgun):** By the time many parents get to the point that they're sitting down and dissecting their child's academic shortcomings, they are armed with a multitude of ammunition (grades, attitude, study habits, and so on) with which they can drive a conversation. Tempting though it may be, it's vital that you don't unload the entire arsenal in one conversation, or even several for that matter. Before you begin the process, make a list of what seems to be the underlying issues that need addressing. It's worth reminding you again that process trumps product. Steamrolling your teen about their report card grades, or exam grades, or quiz scores, does little to drive the conversation toward a productive existence. Conversely, it squashes all productivity in one naggy step. Here are some suggested targeted topics:

☆ **Study habits:** how they are preparing, the amount of time they prepare, where they study, what resources they are utilizing or underutilizing, who they are studying with, etc.

☆ **Communication habits:** how they are communicating (if at all) with their teachers, what they are doing to (actively) seek information or solidify concepts that are giving them trouble.

☆ **Work/play ratio:** the amount of time they spend being social versus time spent delegated to homework, studying, sleeping, working out, etc.

☆ **Long-term goals:** Parents often like to point out what their kids are doing that won't get them to college, but spend less time helping their teen craft what the teen wants for themselves. Attaching academic performance to tangible thoughts like a specific college (even if it's totally unrealistic based on their current results) will heighten that child's efforts. We'll address this with more depth in the communication section of this book.

Next steps: use these categories to craft questions or openers for your sit-downs. Here are some suggestions to drive your conversations to a more positive and productive place:

Avoid saying: You never study!
Instead, ask: How much time do you think you could be spending on your test preparation to earn a B rather than a C?

Avoid saying: Do you even get help from your math teacher?
Instead, say: Let's identify what, exactly, is giving you trouble in math so that we can email your teacher to arrange a meeting for extra help.

Avoid saying: With these grades, you can kiss college goodbye!
Instead, ask: Where would you like to go to college? Let's look up information on that school so that we can see what kinds of classes you need to take in high school, and what grades you should be earning to get admitted.

★ **Change can be messy, slow, painful, and frustrating:** The only thing more painful than change, is staying where you are not meant to be. If you think that your teenager is not where they should be, are meant to be, then buckle up and get ready for a marathon. It's not a sprint. These unhealthy habits, negative mindset, low grades, and lack of confidence are years in the making. Sure, they perhaps only appeared recently in the form of product (grades) but they have been running round the house for years in the form of process (habits). This is where focus of efforts is critical to acknowledge. You cannot change it all at once. Think big rocks first. What's the one aspect of their hot mess that will induce the most change when it changes? For many teenagers it's time management. It's amazing how easy tests become, and how well they perform on them, when they begin preparing two weeks prior as opposed to two days prior. In my work with teens, one of the first activities I do with them is map out how they capture their time. Teens (and most people) like to say they have no time. Everybody has the same amount of time provided to them: 24 hours. How you spend, prioritize, capture that time differentiates successful students from those who are floundering. The moral here is that change is slow, so your frustration must be tethered to a patient rock.

Let's look at this through a metaphor:

You needed some plants. There you are buying your first plant. Upon purchase, it comes with a tiny white insert in the soil telling you exactly how much water and sun it requires. It even discloses how far to plant it from another plant to optimize growth. You soon discover it needs full sun, plenty of water, and the spacing? That's irrelevant as it's your only one. You love the new plant, it really spruces up your apartment; you water it and you make sure it has full sun. Soon, it begins to grow and bloom; and brings you so much joy that low and behold, you want another one. You run to the store, purchase it, and it's slightly different but close enough. However, this time, one minor, innocent, yet significant error has occurred: you disregard the small white insert with the instructions on it. You toss it; your other plant has done so well that you figure why would you need to read that silly card again! The second plant is placed directly next to the first; it's watered similarly, given sun similarly, but it doesn't grow. Hmmm. What's wrong with this plant?! It's alive but not thriving; it's not blooming; it's meek at best and certainly nothing to brag about. What's wrong with it? Nothing. The plant's not the problem; you are. You assumed it was just like the last plant, and it's not.

I know what you're thinking: My children are not plants and you, sir, are not a botanist. Correct. Both times. I am, however, positioned in a job where I interface with many second siblings flailing through high school suffering from the parenting strategies that yielded remarkable results with the family's first child, but are not suitable for the second. If you know much about the role of an assistant principal then you are aware that in large part we interface most with students who are disenfranchised, misguided, misunderstood, mildly to convincingly angry, uninspired, lost, behind, down-and-out. Regardless of what you want to call it or however you want to classify it, they all have something in common: they're trying to get, and most important keep, their parents' attention. The underlying issue? They aren't having their needs met; and it's no one's fault. Commonly, neither parent nor child realize that the previously successful methods and systems that propelled the first child into awesomeness are proving futile on the second go around. Hence the anger. The confrontations. The miscommunication.

Back to plants for a minute: All plants to some degree require water and light to thrive. Right now, in my house, I have plants positioned in different areas according to their needs; they all live in my house, but they are not treated the same. The orchid likes to be left almost entirely alone and same with the succulents (but in a different sort of way); the herbs are needy and high maintenance. I could go on, but you get the point. The same approach needs to be taken into your parenting strategies. Same house, different kids, different needs. A one-sized approach does not work with plants, and certainly is a grave error when raising mentally healthy and vibrant children.

A shift in thinking is required: It's totally normal to compare your children; it has its time, place, and life within the realities of parenting. I urge you to recognize comparisons for data's sake, but strongly advise against verbalizing the contrasts directly to your children. For example, I imagine you know which of your children began to walk or talk earlier than the other, but no one remembers (besides you) who did what first; they each got there eventually. I urge you to celebrate who your second child is for who they are and not for who you were anticipating them to be. Critical life and academic decisions should be driven by maturity and not age or typical hierarchical order. A license may be granted at sixteen but that does not mean every child gets one; and AP Human Geography might be a perfect match for certain ninth graders, but not all. This is particularly important when guiding second siblings through high school; they should not be expected to embrace a sport, activity, or lifestyle simply because it was what was done previously by child number one. It is vital to determine who they are, what they like, what inspires them, and what natural limits are in play, prior to mandating a prescribed path that is both uninspiring to the student and increasingly painful to the health of the relationship between that child and their parents. I am not recommending that you let your child do whatever they want, but I am urging you to let them carve their own slice of the family pie; and do it with their best effort, your full support, and within a well-defined family plan. Communication is key. It is the water and sunlight to your relationship and to their success; without it, they will remain meek and frail. Surviving but not thriving.

Prune as needed: Sometimes plants get too big for their own good, and counterintuitively we need to prune them to their most basic being to ensure long term health; the same is often true with teens. Teens make mistakes, and mistakes need to be addressed. For some reading this analogy, pruning could be taking the keys to the car, or cutting off extra money, or isolating them from their friends, implementing drug testing, making them get a job (the list goes on). Prune away, but do so with caution; prune with clear intent. Prune with a logical plan in order to ensure the long-term health of your teen. A hopeless teen is a dangerous animal. We don't prune a plant by chopping it down; and we can't take a teen out at the knees and expect them to get back up. Be deliberate with your decisions and be willing to adjust according to situational need. More than anything else, prune with unconditional love.

There's a reason gardens have more than one kind of plant: Your second child (or third, or fourth) is their own person, their own plant, with unique qualities, needs, likes, strengths, weaknesses, beauty, size, shape, future and so on; treat them as such. If they seem wilted, try moving them to a new window, or adjust their sunlight, or water. For the same window that gave your first such astounding growth may be unintentionally shading a plant that requires full sun.

PART 4

Proactive & Consistent Parenting

The family castle: You are the parent, king or queen of the family castle. Housing, providing for, and looking after priceless goods in the form of children. One strategy I recommend to parents managing (pre)teenagers is one that I commonly refer to as *parenting down the middle*. Essentially, it's the political equivalent of a liberal Republican or a conservative Democrat. In short, this means neither locking your daughter up in the castle's tallest tower, nor letting her cavort with the alligators in the mote. As a former teacher and high school assistant principal, the statement I've seen *too much* is a grotesque understatement. So, yes, I've been witness to many-a-tale of kids making horrible choices. Kids and horrible choices go hand in hand. But there's a twist. Most of these kids-making-horrible-decisions scenarios come from one of two parenting structures: in the tower or in the mote.

The tower: Tower Kids are kept almost entirely out of the fray, and to an over the top, *no way in hell you're ever going to that party* sort of way. Tower Kids are most often raised in a carefully controlled environment, by cautious, well-intentioned and socially paranoid parents. While parents can successfully raise their Tower Kids (at least in the short term), often Tower Kids end up tying their sheets together and climbing out the window in the middle of the night to check out the mote. Hell bent on asserting their independence and drinking, streaking, or shoplifting their way out from under their overly-protective Tower Parents' iron fists, they go buck-wild the first time their feet hit the damp mud of the mote's shoreline. In short, Tower Kids snap. In part because they simply think they can't take it any longer. They freak out. Overcorrect. Seek new experiences and a bite of the apple.

The mote: Mote Kids live the opposite kind of existence. Rules and modest behavioral expectations are second to *kids will be kids* and *I did that, too,* thereby fostering an environment where anything goes. Or most things, go, anyway. Mote Kids often find themselves raised by two polar-opposite types of family structures. Mote Kids commonly are a product of a single-, over-worked- and overstressed-parent home, where things like curfew live in the shadow of swing shifts and two jobs. Or, they are born into uber-successful and financial-empire-running sets of parents, where details like coming home hammered are lost in the shuffle of a grueling work-travel-jet-lag parent schedule; where coming home too late, or staying home from school for no reason, go largely unnoticed by less judgmental or less likely to act hired help. Mote Kids are hell bent on getting their on-another-business-trip parent's attention by vaping, grossly underperforming academically, getting a sexy lower back tattoo, or hitting up the local bar scene with their new fake ID.

Of course, Tower Kids and Mote Kids are merely composite generalizations, but they do illustrate a point for consideration: extreme parenting, from both sides of the moral aisle, can backfire. Parenting more "down the middle" can help alleviate dramatic episodes and increase the communication channels and mutual respect.

I was nothing short of a Tower Kid. Except, I didn't get all Hell-bent until college; and oh yeah, my parents weren't even there to notice. Nevertheless, I was extremely sheltered from general spontaneous peer-to-peer interaction. And with good cause, really. My impulse control and zest for awkward interactions far exceed that of a normal person my age. I still managed to have uncomfortable run-ins with more of the Mote Kids than I would have preferred, but my tower isolation didn't help the matter.

Parenting is largely based on the example you live: Don't confuse the following chapter with a suggestion or command that you should not drink; unless drinking is holding you back from being your authentic self. But when you openly, or blindly encourage, enable, or simply permit your teenagers to *get ready for college* by getting hammered in your backyard, you're robbing them of the coping skills needed to endure adolescence. More so, if you, yourself are the example, the reference point of normalcy, and it always involves a substance, then you can expect your teen to emulate that in their own life. Even if they don't like anything about you, they will mimic your social tendencies. But when, which more often is the case, they idolize you and respect you and think you are truly the shit (pardon my language), then we have a real issue simmering on the stove. It simmers at 14 years old, and by 17 it's often spilling down the front of the stove, too hot to mop up. I champion you to roll up your sleeves and get under the hood of your soul and look around; identify your positives, negatives, areas of growth, all in a collective effort to be the best version of yourself, and to be the best example for your child. It's hard to parent with a hangover. You know what's harder? Carrying with you any kind of expectation of being taken seriously if your teenager views you as a hypocrite. Whatever that is to you. Do it. Try it. Risk it. Be it. Live it. Don't wait. Your full capacity as a person and parent awaits. So, get after it already!

Engaged and assertive parenting: Conscious parenting is demanding work. Yes, it is tiring. Or I should say, it can be, especially when you have too many rules in play. The more rules one has, the more they must enforce. Wait, what? This doesn't mean that parents should haul off and let teenagers do whatever they please (*like that one parent you're thinking of and judging right now, does*), but I prefer to emphasize general philosophies over a litany of rules. It's going to be much more efficient (I caution using the term easier) to raise a holistically sound, moral, vibrant, college-admissible and summer-job-hireable teenager when they operate from a place where they make decisions based on how that decision fits into their family's value system, rather than the actual rule itself. More of a *I'm gonna go ahead and leave this party where everyone is hammered and taking half-naked selfies and a variety of other horrible decisions are being made* as opposed to *my parents told me if I was ever around anyone drinking they would literally kill me.*

Yes, in the short term, fear from dying due to parent's punishing is effective, but its side effects are many times worse. The iron curtain approach to parenting, where the fear of God is used, and concrete lines are poured into the sand, most certainly always leads to super-shady behavior from the teenagers involved. Elaborate plans are hatched; dishonesty and manipulation rule the roost. Fear of an anywhere-near-beer-induced *killing* by a parent, is far less valuable in the long term than the teen understanding the various ramifications and potential landmines caused by staying in such an environment.

Again, this isn't about me, it's about your parenting. But I will say that while I don't love teenage drinking, and I absolutely believe you can enforce a zero tolerance for consumption policy, it is a reality that at some point, they will be in an anywhere-near-beer situation. Do you want them to be able to divulge that? And talk to you about it? And learn from it? So it's a more balanced approach that is most effective. In college, a parent won't be waiting to *kill* them but the party, with selfies and booze and bad decisions will be exponential. So teaching them why it's not healthy to consume beer, what will happen if they do under your roof etc. is great, but in this training ground you may want them to at least be around it at some point. Confusing, I know.

It takes work and commitment: Being an assertive parent is exhausting. But you know what's worse? Living the reality where half of the time you're an engaged parent, and the other half of the time you're cleaning up the mess made from not being one. Think bail. Or emergency room visits. Or visiting a high school assistant principal to view topless pics of your little, sweet, fourteen-year-old daughter, taken shortly after a few Jell-O shots. And oh yeah, SHE sent the pics! Parents are victims of their own inconsistencies and knee-jerky responses; too often they're shooting from the hip, or they're out of bullets, or they've left their pistol in the car, or they've lost the gun altogether. One day (from the teenager's vantage point at least) there are rules in play, and consequences given, but the next day that same rule is ignored, and the teenager's reality is void of accountability. It's confusing for your teen, and it's a trap for you.

Here's the reality: parents are victims of the rules they don't legitimize, fail to consistently enforce, or don't fully embrace as a united-parental-unit.

Defining a clearly understood family paradigm is essential to raising more aware and (likely) compliant teenagers. Think for a second; what are the core values you hope to instill in your children? What are the values behind the rules you want to establish, enforce, and maintain? The rules are just the conduit, the messenger, for the larger family paradigm. Without you first knowing why you're making said rules, it is impossibly futile to expect a typical teenager to give an eff about your rules. For example, some common values are honesty, integrity, faith, humility, health, and safety. Try to pinpoint three to five. Stay south of five; too many and good luck getting them to stick. Once you have those values defined, apply them to the four categorial sections of this book: school/academics, drugs/alcohol, social media/technology, and family dynamics/communication. The values are the filter through which the categorical sections are strained. It is the goal that your teenager filters their decisions through the value filters prior to making one. And when they don't make the correct decision, which they often won't, despite knowing the values behind it, intervene, punish, or cry-yourself-to-sleep (just kidding). But really, without truly knowing your family paradigm and making it fully understood (as best a teenager can fully understand anything) the next four to six years could end up feeling like, or end up being, ten to twelve years.

Consistency wins: Consistency is the key ingredient to any successful plan of performance. Compounded decisions, made thoughtfully, over time, produce steady teenagers and calmer homes. But this life is crazy-fast and the landscape of your teenager's reality morphs seemingly overnight. Reactive parenting tends to rise to the surface and take the wheel in these fast times. Reactive parenting is not a winning strategy. Proactive, consistent parenting, while initially more challenging and labor intensive to implement, wins.

Examples of reactive parenting:
- Curfews that ebb and flow, change constantly (sometimes it's 10pm and other times it's 11pm—but the variables are identical)
- Rules that allow certain actions under certain circumstances but not others (drinking a few beers is okay at Prom, but not on most weekends)
- Academic-responsibility routines lack structure (student not required to study normally, but grounded and on study-lockdown if they earn a C or lower)
- Consequences and interventions are not discussed until the 11th hour when the ship is sinking (we never discussed what would happen if she smoked vape in the bathroom at school, so we have no plan when she does)

Examples of proactive and consistent parenting:

- Curfews are set, known, planned and enforced
- Expected behaviors, no-nos, infractions are expressed, clear and simple
- Academics are prioritized and how, when, where, why they take place are known, clearly structured, and kept in check
- Parents discuss the what-ifs, have created a crib-sheet of responses to said hypotheticals so to be fluid in their response when they finally occur—and don't have to wait for the other parent to get home before issuing a consequence

Mixed messages: When parenting is rooted in reactive tones and practices, it causes longer, more dramatic and more confusing moments for both teenagers and parents. Like it or not, just as parents love to track the details of past teenager decisions, mistakes, choices etc., so, too, do teenagers track past parenting choices of their parents when looking for leverage.

A mixed message in real-life: I knew a high school teen who disagreed with their parents about attending a party. The teen was not allowed to go (responsible choice by the parents given the circumstances surrounding the party) and the teen was very angry. This conflict led to a series of conflicts and caused significant turmoil within the household. By the time that I spoke with the teen, which was several days later, they were still upset. My instinct was to defend the parents; I began pontificating about the dangers of the party. Politely, they let me finish. It turns out, the teen was not in disagreement with the rationale for why the party was unsafe; they could see the elements of the party that were not suitable for a teenager. The issue was that their parents had previously allowed them to attend other parties, or take other adventures with friends that were (in their teen mind) equally unsafe. Thus, the parents had created an expectation that they were able to handle those situations. The teen was mad because their parents were not being consistent, they were being ambiguous, and teenagers don't do well in ambiguity. Their parent-fence was missing boards.

What mixed messages are you giving to your teen:

Mixed message:
Mixed message:
Mixed message:
Mixed message:
Mixed message:

Getting real for the sake of our teenagers: I understand and sympathize with the fact that many people are not intentionally being fake, or false, or pretend; they are simply being. This is crucial when understanding teenagers. In fact, with the thick and complicated layers of teenagedom, comprised of friendships, romantic interests, frenemies, homework, visiting nana in the desert, and whether or not it's their day to walk the dog they begged for two Christmases ago, teenagers are so busy surviving that not much of what they do is super intentional. Simply being involves so many split-second and long-term life choices all at once, that teens don't necessarily choose much. Teens aren't exactly experiencing a free will in the way adults do. For many teenagers, arguably most, the decision-making process (however dismal it is) hinges on nothing more than trying to find the path of least resistance. Teenagers have lots of resistance in their lives. Some of it good, and some of it bad. They have resistance from peers, resistance from social norms and pressures, resistance from the adults in their lives (however well intentioned), to name a few sources. The multitude of resistors is exhausting, and simply stated, teens begin to lose their footing and get carried away by the current of life. Metaphorically, for some reason, I'm often drawn to the somewhat cliché of a stream: specifically, swimming up it versus being carried by it.

This is where, as parents, you must thread the needle between understanding the teenage paradigm and enabling it. It's vital to understand some basics in terms of teenage social and academic motivators, but equally important to not become part of the machine of enablement. We must acknowledge the teenage paradigm, and parlay that understanding into action; actions of support for our teenagers. Today's teenagers are going through the motions as they understand them to be at that specific moment in time. It's a matter of social survival. This is not to admonish the teens from accountability over their choices, or to say that they are hapless victims who can't be expected to decide. Not the case. Really, though, I am offering the suggestion that although teenagers do have a backbone, they really need the adults in their lives to act as the muscle tissue that surrounds the backbone. Teenagers lack the proper muscle to walk tall. To stand in their truth. To thrive. We as adults must flex our muscle, both actively and subtly, to allow the teenager to fully develop into their true being and usher shades of authenticity into their palette.

Examples of enabling teenagers:

- Allowing your teen to stay home, sick, based on poor time management that resulted in not finishing an essay.

- Calling your teen "out sick" so they can attend a music festival, and in the process, miss a test.

- Giving in to a later curfew time when your teenager begs you via text to stay out for just one more hour.

- Accepting your teen's lowered standards (below their capabilities within normal efforts).

Where are you enabling your teen?

Enablement:
Enablement:
Enablement:
Enablement:
Enablement:

Being a teenager is difficult, but that's not reason to skip that phase of life: If I had a dollar for each time a parent dropped some version of the old adage *it used to be so simple when I was a teenager,* or *I wouldn't want to be a teenager today*, I most likely wouldn't be writing this book. Or maybe I would be, but from my own secluded island after a quick scuba with Sir Richard Branson. You see, a large part of the teenage authenticity identity crisis is parent created. Adulting is hard work. And being a passive adult is far easier and more rewarding (initially) than that of a more rigid or moral-driven adult peer. But I get it. Some of the sell-outness of adults letting teens shotgun cans of beer in the backyard is guilt or burden driven. Adults seemingly pity or feel bad for today's youth. They point towards technology, and social media, and politics, and the environment ... and that pity leads to loose, entitlement-heavy parenting. Not to burst the bubble of the cool parent on the corner, but all your Nelly remixes and Jell-O shots at your 16-year-old teen's birthday party isn't going to change any of that. Any of it. In fact, what all that, and other misguided acts of enablement, do is rob that same pitied youth of the structure, fortitude, and coping skills that they so desperately need to navigate this crazy world.

I don't live under a rock; I am acutely aware that the world today is changing at the speed of a fiber optic internet connection. And many of those changes can in fact be, without a doubt, categorized as bad change. But call me blind, as I fail to see the connection between negative social evolution and railroading teens toward the rabbit hole of addiction, technological dependency, and utter delusion within the context of personal accountability. Despite this high rate of change and social evolution and technological advances, it is vital to acknowledge that the fundamental needs of teenagers are still operating with a dial-up connection. Teens have four basic needs: food, shelter, love, and structure. With those they can conquer the world; really.

Advantages of being a teen today?	Disadvantages of being a teen today?

Just as I wrote this book, I assume you're reading because you're not ready to throw in the towel in the fight against the faux-life being peddled to our youth. I wrote this book because I'm simply not down with high school parents being drinking buddies. Or with clicky-mom-BFFs posturing as mean girls, and cyber bullying their neighbors or the attendance technician at the local high school. I'm not down with the normalization of an academia absent from integrity. Or the expectation that parents must either choose for their teen to be popular or live a healthy and drug-free lifestyle. I wrote this book because I see too many parents who parent their teenagers from a fear-driven paradigm. They fear their own children. And I can relate to that fear.

Why adults are intimidated by teenagers: When I began to teach, I lived in constant fear of my students. I wanted them to like me. To love me. To accept me as the resident expert. I wanted them to follow my rules. To respect me. And over time, my students did most of those things, most of the time. But after all, they were twelve. But honestly, the fact that a grown professional is ever genuinely fearful of twelve-year-olds (which I was) shows you just how powerful kids can be, and how the dynamics between a parent and child can get so complicated. Those fearful feelings were tenfold when I assumed the role of assistant principal of a high school. That was fear fest 2012. I was horrified. The days of being the cool teacher were over. Now I had to be the one delivering the sad news, the consequences, the high expectations, the formalities of all things good and bad in a high school. And in that role, there were some very big burdens to carry. It was like I was the bellhop: organizing, sorting and storing their baggage, helping them relocate it, load or unload it ... and sometimes I would get tipped, and sometimes I wouldn't.

Assertive, intelligent, well-educated, motivated, scared, nervous, and cornered or competitive teenagers are horrifying. The trick is leaning into that sense of horror, walking with confidence, and not letting them see the fear in your eye. Basically, make it until you fake it. Largely, teenagers are only really scary at first. They wanted to see where I stood. What I stood for. *How much resolve do you, Mr. New Assistant Principal, have?* I was fearful they would see that I was afraid. I was fearful they would not like me and key my car and say nasty things about me on social media. They did all of those, by the way. I was fearful that they would revolt and simply not listen to me ... and then what would I do? I was fearful that students would discover that I really found quite a bit of humor in and appreciation for their antics. They did. Mostly, being an administrator was just about four years of *what the hell am I doing right now* combined with *this is the best job anyone would ever want or need.*

The key point to understand in this example of my fear-based entry into both teaching and administration is that I did not let the fear impact my job performance. Sure, I was scared often, and anxious, but I did not let that stop me from doing what I knew was best for kids. And their parents. Even when students, parents, families etc., did not agree with me or could not see the value in my actions or decisions, I was confident in my choices. I didn't always like the message that had to be delivered, but it got delivered. Sure, would I have preferred that they didn't come to a football game hammered? Yes. Would I have preferred they would have simply done their homework versus ordering the teacher's edition online and distributing it to all their peers? Yep. The list goes on. But my role, my part in the *adulting* happening at the school level was to treat these hiccups as learning opportunities. And sometimes the only way to deliver that lesson is with gloves off (metaphorically, of course).

How I conquered teenage intimidation:

★ **Integrity:** As a teacher and administrator there is a constant undercurrent between what should be done, needs to be done, and the path of least resistance. It became clear very quickly that teenagers are savvy and were willing to work me to get what they wanted. I had to focus on actions that were suited for the teens' best long-term interests, education, and health, as opposed to whether they were comfortable or agreeable with those decisions or feedback.

★ **Honesty:** As an adult charged with educating and maintaining the physical and mental health of hundreds, or thousands of teenagers, it was important that I assumed the expert or authority position within the relationship—but equally important was not marching around as if I had the answer or perfect solution for any question or scenario. Teens appreciate authority when it is presented in a cerebral and meaningful way. Sometimes that meant being perfectly upfront about my lack of expertise or finite knowledge. In the same vein, I focused on consistently articulating my appreciation, concern, pride, disappointment, or enthusiasm in their lives.

★ **Confidence:** If you can't make it, fake it. I was totally intimidated when I became a teacher, and then twofold upon landing a role as an assistant principal. Teenagers are drawn to confidence, partly because they are constantly struggling with their own. Maintaining an outwardly confident posture and mindset was a must. Stand up straight. Look them in the eye. Know their names. Smile. Laugh. Have a real conversation beyond school and grades. Teens are ever-evaluating and assessing those around them for signs and manifestations of self-confidence. Those who exude it possess a greater likelihood in gaining their respect and (for lack of a better word) compliance.

★ **Reflection:** Working in a school setting is a bit like Ground Hog's Day. Round and round, you go, with slight changes to the details of each day, but within a large, much-predicable shell. Reflection is a slippery slope as too much negative self-feedback can stump the very confidence required to be successful with teenagers; not enough, and you lose humility and grow cocky. I focused on learning from my mistakes, miscalculations: times when I was too firm, or not nearly firm enough. This continual reflection allowed me to sharpen my game and improve the productivity of each new day, month, and year.

★ **Professional growth:** Nothing changes if nothing changes. New information and research is ever-flowing regarding best practices on leadership, the teenage brain, and teaching strategies. I read. Constantly. And still do. Part of my professional growth though, with teenagers, was not available in a book, or the Internet; it was only available from the source themselves, teenagers. Teenagers are experts in their own world, trends, pressures, expectations, interest points: all aspects that one who wants to have positive influence or meaningful and responsible relationships with teenagers should know if they want to continue or maximize their positive role in that teen's life.

Circling back to fear. Many parents fear their teenagers. No question. Teenagers can be horrifying. Moody. Mad. Mean. Dramatic. Unreasonable. Irrational. Emotional. Defiant. So just as the teens filter what they might do, or not do, based on their anticipated reaction by the adults in their lives, so, too, do adults. Only in reverse order. Recapping: teens weigh the cost benefit between their proposed action (i.e., drinking booze) with the social prowess and enjoyment it will bring them versus the consequences and scrutiny it might render. On the flip side of this coin are the adults. Many parents are acutely aware of their teenager's actions, but do nothing.

Side effects of being a scared parent:

★ **You hide from confrontation:** Many parents can easily rattle off a laundry list of "issues" they would love to broach with their teenager, but don't. Increasingly, parents grow weary from confrontation and find it easier to say nothing at all, than engage in a potentially hostile, tough, messy, and emotional conversation. That short-term fix creates a much larger, longer-term problem. As one issue remains in limbo, causing palpable tension within the home, sure as rain, another arrives, and another, and another ... until it is total madness.

★ **Your teenager assumes the dominant power position in the house:** The biggest, most negative compounding consequence from parents' lack of confrontation, is a shift of power. A common example is parents who attempt to confront an issue, say curfew, but are met with a huge offensive from their teenager. Emotional rage and mean, nasty comments spew from the lips and effectively overwhelms the fight within the parents. They exhaust, out-yell and outlast the parents. I am not encouraging you to have drop-down drag-out shouting matches with your child; but know that when you consistently back down, a new order emerges where the teen is driving the ship.

★ **You don't make decisions you want to because you're scared:**
Within this on-going progression, the parent shies away from
ruling the roost. The final piece is when your lack of will
turns to a constant feeling of fear. You become scared of your
own child. You are afraid of what they are doing (or not doing), you find yourself unable to confront them; when you
do, you can't hang, and you become paralyzed: unable to
parent.

An example in real life: I worked with a family who was suspicious
that their teen was engaging in drug use.

In the context of their management plan they implemented
a drug test. Sounds obvious, right? Yes, in theory, a drug test is
wonderful; it provides parents with the ammunition and information needed to act and respond appropriately to either
suspected or known drug use. However, tools like drug tests are
messy and somewhat paralyzing when the parents aren't clear
with themselves, and with their teens, as to what that action or
response to a positive drug test will be. In fact, with drug tests,
parents often cross the subtle threshold between ignorance and
enablement. It's one thing when a parent suspects their teen is
using, but takes no vested or active interest in finding out, and
quite another when the same parent has tangible information,
yet chooses to do nothing with it.

It is absolutely a must for parents to evaluate what potential
actions their teen may take, and then not only surmise what
their own response to the teen's action will be, but dial in and
determine exactly what steps (actions) they will take in response.
As for the family that I was working with, the drug test elicited a
typical response. When the results came in, and listed several
drugs (from soft, to hard, to prescription) paralysis ensued.
While it would have been easy to qualify their lack of action as
not caring, in fact, it was a direct result of the void of forethought
and preparation staring them in the face. The parents hadn't
anticipated a positive result; especially for hard drugs. And drugs
that weren't prescribed. Thus, they had not formulated their

action plan. This lack of planning caused a significant lag time in both the efficiency with which they responded as well as in their ability to maintain composure (if only for show) in front of their child. During debriefing in a later session, what they verbalized was interesting. They admitted to in fact expecting marijuana, and had already subconsciously attached an *I did marijuana when I was teenager; at least it's not something worse.* But it was something worse; two something worses.

Not caring and not knowing what to do are two separate states of parental being. But the validity of parental paralysis as a viable excuse has an extremely short shelf life. Like it or not, every parent has a level of responsibility attached to teens' actions. This may be purely reputational all the way to full legal liability. Many parents neglect to zoom out to see how the actions can result in tangible damage, far from the typical headache and angst of raising a teenager. The good news is that by shifting to a slightly more engaged parenting model, you can create and communicate the clarity required to significantly decrease a major landmine on your teen's road to adulthood.

Where are you frozen in your parenting?
(issues you won't or don't confront)

Frozen:
Frozen:
Frozen:
Frozen:
Frozen:

Tips for anticipating teenage landmines

★ Communicate with your insurance provider to obtain a list of clinicians who specialize in teenage mental health and substance use.

★ Talk to your insurance provider about coverage for in- and outpatient programs.

★ Research local parent support opportunities. This might be your own clinician, family coach, or support group that can better equip you to not only address the variety of challenges thrown your way, but to do it with the understanding that you are not in it alone.

★ Brainstorm a list of actions (think big and gnarly) and see what your instincts tell you as to how you might confront, triage, and remedy them.

★ Notice where you freeze and want to quit the activity. This paralysis is the threshold of plausible deniability; fight through it and try to confront these scenarios anyhow.

★ Talk to older parents who have a parenting model you respect: pick their brains, listen to their war stories, and gain insight from those who have been there, done that.

★ Read. Read. Read. There are countless books, like this one, intended to plant seeds of assertion, confidence, and action in parents. Hop online and order a few. See what sticks.

Indeed, a quagmire of factors have made fostering a teenager's authentic spirit more challenging, less rewarding, and at most times, an uphill battle. And? We need to stop whining about it on Facebook already and act. I remain steadfast in my optimism that through trickle down, authenticity-building, assertive, strategically-engaged parenting, parents can and will positively shape the lives of teenagers. Basically, if your teenager views you as one of the most annoying humans you're onto something. Of course, this annoyance is only applicable if it's because you won't let them get wasted in your living room, or permit them to cheat on exams or berate less educated blue-collar workers at the mall. It, however, is void, if it's because you're getting hammered in your living room, stirring the neighborhood gossip, or sending your Halibut back with a bad attitude. If they know your love for them is greater than your *pushoverness*, and that you actively parent with a longer view than weekend plans, the *I hate yous* of today will eventually evolve into the *thank yous* of college graduations, first jobs, and weddings. But it's gonna suck. A ton. At first at least. Yes, it would be easier to acquiesce and be reality-show cool ... but if the plan is to stop parenting them at the teenager level eventually, then assertive parenting is key. No, I don't think you need to lock them in the castle tower, but I also know that you don't want them getting lit with the alligators in the mote, either. Somewhere between the two is ideal. I don't know what you call that in a castle (I didn't think through that metaphor all the way I guess). Regardless, you want them on the main level of the castle with access to the draw bridge.

How fear is affecting your parenting: Through the course of my own personal development, including work with my coach Anney, I have grown to understand and appreciate the importance of fear. Fear is both a formidable adversary and an extremely powerful energy source, which, when channeled, produces the necessary energy to tackle even the most daunting tasks—such as parenting. Part of my new reality involves the daily practice, really the moment-to-moment practice, of leaning into or feeling into my fears. By noticing fear, I am more equipped to understand the impact fear has on my life. Fear works by either producing negative actions, or by preventing positive actions. Noticing fear allows me to better understand how it is affecting my mind, decision-making processes and overall wellness. I have discovered the sooner I give a peanut to the fear-mongering elephant in the corner of my office, the sooner said elephant leaves my space, thereby freeing up room for productive and positive thoughts, words, and actions.

Let's take a closer look at fear in the context of parenting teenagers. When parenting teenagers, parents respond to their parental fears by either engaging in actions they normally would not (negative behaviors) or avoid proactive or assertive parental actions altogether (positive actions) to avoid conflict. This concept can be misleading; many positive actions taken by assertive and present parents are not at all pleasant, and thus wouldn't normally be associated with the concept of positivity.

Fear is constantly fighting and jockeying to be the alpha emotion of parenting. Unfortunately, emotional hierarchy has placed fear *second* to love, and this really irritates the hell out of fear. Like an annoying child, it is constantly tapping, and interrupting, and making plays for your attention. As parents, when we ignore the fear we are experiencing, we only delay the inevitable knockdown, drag-out conflict that is being kicked down the parental road. Many parental emotions are fear driven. Being sad, frustrated, nervous, angry, or lonely are often merely shades of parental fear. As such it is vital to notice your fear. Acknowledge it. And then let it guide you into potentially positive actions. Where fear wants to wallow, we must problem solve. Where fear wants to complain about the rain, we need to jump into the puddles with rain boots.

How is it impacting your life? What actions is fear creating (negative actions) and what is it stopping (positive actions)?

Confronting your fear.

List: your smaller scale fears regarding your teenagers and being their parent. These fears may be about your teenagers directly, or more indirectly centered on you. Example: *I fear my teenager's angry-drunk personality when he comes home on Saturday nights* or *I'm afraid if I don't allow my teen to go to parties like his buddies do, he soon won't get invited anywhere and have buddies.*

Small fear 1:
Small fear 2:

| Small fear 3: |
| Small fear 4: |
| Small fear 5: |

List: your bigger-picture parental fears: the ones that may take time to unfold. Example: *I'm afraid my teenager won't get into a good college. Or, I'm afraid my teenager will drop out of college like I did.*

| Big fear 1: |
| Big fear 2: |
| Big fear 3: |
| Big fear 4: |
| Big fear 5: |

Notice: What are these fears stopping you from doing (**positive actions**)? Example: *I don't confront my teens about their drinking—it's not worth the drama. They won't listen.*

| Action 1: |
| Action 2: |

Action 3:
Action 4:
Action 5:

Notice: What are these fears causing you to do (**negative actions**)? Example: *I allow my teen to drink with friends so that they can be popular. I hold it all in and then SCREAM obscenities rather than having a proper heart-to-heart talk.*

Action 1:
Action 2:
Action 3:
Action 4:
Action 5:

Redirect: What action would you prefer to do? What do you know you should do differently? What do you need to change to do this? What small actions can you implement to get closer to a more assertive role?

New Action 1:
New 2:

New 3:
New 4:
New 5:

The sooner you readily welcome your fears, as strange and counterintuitive as that sounds, the more quickly you can move on from them. Of course, simply noticing your fears will not make them go away, but it will change your relationship with them, and allow you to regain the position, power, and progress that has been stymied along the way.

Clarify your perspective to declutter your parenting: Just as there are a myriad of distractions, technological advances, and social media platforms that have made the road to authenticity hard to pave, these same potholes can be turned into invaluable resources in the war on complicit parenting. Parents today have access to the necessary resources needed to create a foundation for their children to thrive. They can use the basic approaches of unemotional, consistent, and leverage-based parenting that can and will produce meaningful, positive, nostalgia-heavy memories for their children.

Parents have the chance to properly equip their children with both the emotional and the pragmatic tools needed to leave the home, go to college, stay at college, and perhaps even get a real job soon. But it takes work. And effort. And rules. And structure. And tough love. And disappointment. And alienation. And looking like an unreasonable or out-of-touch asshole at times. Whatever. These, and other factors, it seems, have influenced many parents to adopt a mindset and parenting paradigm where they simply don't want to put in the work required to ensure that their teen has the best odds at living a healthy, authentic, and mentally vibrant life. You do not have to be one of those parents. And if you are one, or were one, you have the power to change your approach and the course of your teen's life.

What are the core values you want to instill in your teenager?

Core value 1:
Core value 2:
Core value 3:
Core value 4:
Core value 5:

Authenticity: Now seems like an appropriate juncture to pause and clarify my concept of authentic. Certainly, it would be easy to misinterpret my definition of authenticity based on the implications of the previous paragraphs. No, authentic doesn't mean sober, phone-free, home-by-nine, straight-As. Unless it does. I am not suggesting a version of authentic that only includes kids who are both drama- and joint-free, as there will be points in teenagehood at which teens will be the trifecta: dramatic, high, and authentic. Conversely, many of the sketchiest moments a teen escapes will be the most formative lessons they will learn. Every child has a predetermined design that the Universe or God (or whatever you want to call it) has in store for them. Our job is not to confuse their plan with our own. Our job, as the adults in their lives, either as parents, or teachers, or coaches or therapists etc., is to guide them. We need to allow for, create, and implement the proper structure necessary to become their best version.

So back to authentic for a minute. Admittedly, adults cannot manipulate or control all the variables in our children's lives, especially when it comes to teenagers. Look for example, the negative connotation that is associated with parents who society feels are too heavily involved in their children's lives: we refer to them as helicopter parents. This isn't about locking our teenagers up and throwing away the key. Or searching the entire Google search history to connect the trail of breadcrumbs of typical teenage sketchiness. Adults can, however, limit their teenager's access to variables that are out of the scope and sequence appropriate for their age and stage. (By now you might be noticing that I toggle back and forth between the term parent and the term adult. This is a team effort. Parents cannot and will not be effective in isolation. Adulting and parenting are team sports.) Why would we allow for more complicated lessons when the less complicated learning hasn't yet occurred? Imagine if your child was assessed on advanced concepts in math without having been provided the requisite instruction? You would fly your helicopter straight over the school, land it in the quad, and high tail it into the administration building. So why can we expect different outcomes from our children in life? Many of today's most notable landmines to our youth are experiences or substances that they simply are not physiologically or psychologically ready to handle, process, learn from, or be handed on a silver platter.

What makes your teenager authentic?

Trait 1:
Trait 2:
Trait 3:
Trait 4:

Trait 5:

One common, tired, and weak excuse I hear over and over from enable-junky parents is that they want their teen to have whatever experience in a controlled environment, while at home, before they leave for college, so that they know how to handle it. Okay, let's go with that mindset for a bit. Admittedly, there are aspects to that, and similar statements, which are true: *if* those experiences are played out in full. Spoiler: they never are. What occurs (most of the time, that is) is that the parents allow their teen to have said experience, but ultimately wedge their parent-self between their teen and most forms of accountability when that experience goes sideways.

So, the parent wants their teen to learn how to drink before college. They fear they'll rush a Greek house and not be able to get through the hazing or party scene. Forget how screwed up that is in and of itself, that the parent wants the teens to learn how to get hammered ... but let's roll with it for a second. So, they let their teen and friends throw dice on the ping pong table in the back yard. Day drinking quickly turns gnarly, and the teens are wasted before they can tell what happened. The topper? It's a Sunday. And on Monday morning the teen, a senior in high school has a calculus exam. At 8:00 a.m. And if they get a B or lower on said test, they'll end the semester with D. Gasp.

Where are you accelerating your teen's life experiences with weak parenting?

Example 1:

Example 2:

Example 3:

Example 4:
Example 5:

Teenager communication skills run low: Many teenagers have poor communication skills; particularly with their parents. While frustrating, this roadblock is an opportunity to unearth hidden channels of communication without succumbing to unnecessary expenditures of stress or emotion.

Reflect on your current communication channel: First, take a minute to evaluate your current level of communication with your teen. Is it non-existent? Fully transparent? Or leaning to one side or the other? Make no mistake, teenagers will always keep their parents at arm's length, but there are strategies to get them to bend that arm. To know where you're heading, you must know where you are.

Bridging the communication gap with your teenager

Self-assessment: Rate your level of communication with your teenager:

- ○ Awesome
- ○ Strong
- ○ Okay
- ○ Poor
- ○ Ugly
- ○ Nonexistent

Check any topics that you can currently discuss with your teenager:

- ○ Drug Use
- ○ Alcohol Use
- ○ Grades
- ○ Healthy friendships

- Family roles
- Big family decisions, like a move
- Goals and expectations (grades, college, work)
- Hopes and dreams
- Your work or career
- Your family's financial picture and college
- Your marriage or divorce
- Their dating and relationships
- Sex
- Your regrets from adolescence
- Their positive qualities
- Fears: yours and theirs
- Faith and religion

Check any topics that would like to be able to discuss:
- Drug Use
- Alcohol Use
- Grades
- Healthy friendships
- Family roles
- Big family decisions, like a move
- Goals and expectations (grades, college, work)
- Hopes and dreams
- Your work or career
- Your family's financial picture and college
- Your marriage or divorce
- Their dating and relationships
- Sex
- Your regrets from adolescence
- Their positive qualities
- Fears: yours and theirs
- Faith and religion

What first? Which of the above topics is most critical to discuss with your teen? Remember you must cash in a lot of casual conversation equity to generate the income to pay for one critical conversation ... plan and be thoughtful.

The 45-minute rule: If you take only one tip from this chapter, let it be this: when your teen gets home from school, or you from work, do not talk to them *about school* for 45 minutes. This will be impossible for many of you. Set a timer. And no, you may not simply ignore them; but rather, engage in topics other than school. Why? If you don't allow your teen the real estate to decompress after their day, they will avoid you at all costs, and your conversations will be short, contentious, and irritating.

Imagine if after your work day you were expected to immediately rehash it with your teen.

"Why didn't you meet that deadline?" or "Your boss did what?!" or "You need to go in and ask them if there's anything else you can do to earn that bonus!" You couldn't do it. Neither can they.

When I return home, while I'm excited to see my family, I'm in no way ready to review or defend or even celebrate my day. At least not at first. I need time to find the way down to me. To settle. And, your teen requires similar decompression.

Questions to avoid:

✓ How was school?

✓ What did you do at school today?

✓ Do you have any homework?

✓ How did you do on (insert test, quiz, presentation, project)?

Try these instead:

✓ Tell me about your day.

✓ Where did you feel the most successful today?

✓ What was your biggest challenge today?

✓ What made you laugh today?

Look for ways to reach your teen: Everyone has a trigger; the challenge is finding it when it comes to your teen. Discovering this will largely occur through trial by fire. It may be a topic, a subject, a team, a memory, a game, a space, an activity, or an event. The goal as the parent is to persevere long enough to find that connection. For me, as a teen, it was tennis. Tennis was the safe, neutral space where my dad and I could communicate and interact regardless of the current state of our relationship. It was known (without being stated) that when we talked or played tennis, it was civil, polite, and friendly, even if we were none of those things in any other context. You are the parent; you have a premium vantage point and the proximity, and thus, are best positioned to uncover and dig for potential topics, outings, events, activities, sports, games, or memories that will disarm and engage your teen. But discovery is a process.

Go slow to go fast: Haste makes waste. It's vital that you're not peppering your teenager with a myriad of topics for the same reasons the *45-minute rule* is in play. Too much, too soon, or too often will drive them away. Plan; brainstorm your first approach. Pick one avenue, commit to it, and see how it goes. Use that as a barometer; for example, if the attempt was talking about sports, and it flopped, opt for an experience for your second attempt: instead of talking about sports, go watch one.

Use the power of silence to elicit words from your teenager: One extremely obvious but often overlooked fact about kids is that they hate silence. They want to fill it with noise. So, here's a tip for your next car ride: try no music, no parent questions and no mobile device ... the product will be somewhere from a few words to a full-blown conversation; I don't care if they're 5 or 15 years old. When the car is filled with silence, the weight of it sits on their chest and forces out words. Any words. They. Can't. Help. It.

Don't smother your teenager in communication: Often the words generated by the desperation of silence are defensive and mean, or funny and dismissive, but every so often they are a glance straight into their soul. The trade off is worth its weight in Bit-coin (*is that a thing?*). I would love to possess the secret to skipping the meanness and dismissive snipes, but I can't. The first two eventually lead to the last: open communication. Process over product. To achieve relevant and honest channels of communication with your child, you must practice the process of talking. And no one wants to talk to Debbie-Downer (*ya know, with those grades you're not going to get anywhere in life ...*) and no one wants to hear you brag about your glory days (*ya know, when I was in school I played three sports and had a 9.0*), so stop it already.

Some of you reading this are positively thinking: *hey guy, my kid would sit in silence with me for eternity.* Point well taken; but, what are you doing about it? Why won't they talk to you? It's not just because they're a teen; lots of teens talk to their parents. What else could it be? Did something happen? Divorce? Older sibling left for college? Maybe they were kicked out of their friend group. Those answers should help guide you as to where to look for someone to hear them speak. Because if they won't talk to you, it is vital to find someone they *will* talk to. Maybe it's their favorite uncle, or a coach, or a teacher, or a neighbor. Perhaps in elevation of crisis, it's a therapist. Regardless, identifying that they need a listening ear, painful as it is to admit that the person isn't you, is a critical step in helping them open up. Just because that person isn't you now, does not mean it can't and won't be you in the future.

Excuses are the worst, and there exist endless reasons that you have poor communication with your teenager: *they're busy, you never see them, they won't talk to you;* endless reasons exist to explain how the channel of communications has collapsed. *Whoa-is-me will not do anything here.* There are no victims, only volunteers. Create opportunity where there is none. What can you do to let the pressure of silence work in your favor and pro-duce words from your teen? Where can you take them? Only you know that. But I would recommend golf over a movie, or a hike over shopping. Something long enough to generate enough silence, that will in turn produce the first brick in your road of reconnection and communication.

Shelve the shame: There is a lot of pressure to appear to be a perfect or capable parent. But communication breakdowns are painful, and many find embarrassment in them. There should be no shame in reaching out to your people, your parent friends for help and advice. Plenty of parents do in fact communicate well and often with their teens; pick their brains, ask how they do it, seek suggestions like you do for other things, like a good Thai restaurant or landscaper. I find the best answer is typically in the room—only asking for advice will get you options and suggestions to try.

Patience is a weapon, too: Establishing or reestablishing open lines of communication with teenagers takes time; it's not easy and it's tempting to give up. Don't. When they were little, and they threw a fit, you let them kick and scream and cry on the kitchen floor. In time, their fit passed. Now, they're big kids, and instead of the kitchen floor, the fits are silent, passive aggressive, mean or hostile forms of communication. Remember, they're still kids and patience is your best weapon.

Contain your excitement upon a breakthrough: You did it! Your teen finally engaged with you. You found a strategy that disarmed and engaged them. Perfect. Now, don't blow it by immediately getting into the weeds and talking heavy talk. Invest in simple conversations, build equity, and cash it in for the real talk in critical moments. The objective is increased frequency of communication outside of intense or critical or important conversations. So, go you! You're communicating; now build on that success and ride the wave of momentum to a healthier relationship with your child.

Don't be alarmed: It is very typical for teenagers to have poor communication skills with their parents. While this is frustrating, it is critical to find a work around, and not allow that roadblock to cause unnecessary stress or emotion.

Directions: In the boxes provided, fill in potential topics, outings, events, activities, sports, games, memories, teams etc., which might allow your teen to disarm.

Potential icebreakers

Approach 1
Approach 2
Approach 3
Approach 4

Decide: Which of the above approaches will you attempt first? Pick one, commit to trying it, and see how it goes. Record in the box below what your first approach will be.

I'll try this:

Keep in mind: Establishing or reestablishing an open line of communication with teenagers takes time; it's not easy and it's tempting to give up. Don't. When they were little, and they threw a fit, you would let them kick and scream and cry on the kitchen floor. Now, they're big kids, and instead of the kitchen floor, the fit is often silent, passive aggressive, mean, and hostile at times. Remember, they're still kids. Patience is your best weapon.

The value of good listening: Teenagers are talked at all day long, in school, at practice, by the tutor, or coach, or teacher, or bus driver, etc. Many teens develop an aversion to adults because they will either be talked at, and expected to listen, or be asked irrelevant or big questions that they have no idea how to answer.

Teen trigger: ill-informed parent questions:

● **Parents repeating the same basic, foundational questions:** If every conversation begins with questions that have been answered several times already, you will decrease your teen's willingness to engage with you. This pertains to topics like their friends, teachers, and classes.
  ○ *Who's Becky again?*
  ○ *What's your history teacher's name?*
  ○ *You know, your math class, what level is it again?*
  ○ *Wait, I forget, what team are you on?*
  ○ *I'm confused, what season is it? Lacrosse or soccer?*

I get it, you're busy, and they're hard to keep up with. But I strongly suggest being low-key proactive. Take notes, make a flow chart, login to the parent portal on the school website, rehash with your better-informed spouse, or even another sibling; whatever you do, work smarter in your parenting. A bit of homework on your end will expedite conversations and keep them going by avoiding teenage frustrations coming to a boil before they have time to answer the *real* questions you are seeking.

In education, you listen, a lot. Being an assistant principal is not sexy, at all. People are in your office when they're angry, desperate, out of options, only seeing you so they can see the actual principal, in trouble, in tears; they "can't even" or they've just been "rolled." Whatever the case, the assistant principal's office is not typically a place to take refuge. Or at least it was not when I began that role. One strategy I employed to weather, how should I say this, less uplifting times, was to shift back to my own experience in high school. I hated high school, high school hated me, so let's make it different for someone else. I sought to balance out my historical negatives with present positives. I tried each day to create an environment that gave students the best opportunity to reach their full potential in a healthy, happy, and authentic way. I enjoyed nothing more than my time with our students, and within that, listening to them.

It's amazing that I was not fired for lack of paperwork completion, for I had effectively and immediately replaced the time and energy it took to do paperwork with student meetings. Students arrived to my office perhaps out of necessity (*I need my detention cleared; I was given a referral; I was caught plagiarizing*). I am not suggesting they all enjoyed meeting with me, as many did not, and that was made very clear via social media or old school sharpie on the bathroom wall smack talk. But, in each meeting, I relied heavily on a strategy that is often missing in adult to teen communication: unobstructed listening. I listened. For a long time. And then, when and if I said something, it was (if possible) a question. Kids love to talk about themselves. And if they don't ... something is up, and it's bad. Amazing things happen when an assistant principal of a high school takes unlimited student meetings, and primarily listens: they get all the dirt. And the dirt they don't get can be connected easily by the breadcrumbs from earlier meetings. Some of my biggest breakthroughs came from listening.

The more you want to know teenagers, the more you need to engage in unobstructed listening.

Tips for unobstructed listening:

★ **Listen as if you 100% believe everything they're saying:** reserve outward judgement or belief levels for another conversation. For now, simply listen, and note their perspective. Put yourself in their shoes—as if you have never met them and they are telling you this for the first time.

★ **Don't give advice or commentary:** The hardest part about unobstructed listening is resisting the temptation to insert your own personal anecdotes or opinions. When you interject, the talk becomes a comparison between their reality, and yours. It showcases the divide between the two of you. By simply listening, you preserve ownership for them, and the more they own the conversation, the more they'll say.

★ **Articulate your active listening with expressions of sympathy, empathy, and belief:** Of course, you shouldn't just sit there in dead silence while they talk and talk. They might think you're not interested or listening. Small statements of affirmation and understanding suggest engagement and allow you to further expand the talk. Now don't haul off with over-the-top, inauthentic hems and haws. Be simple and succinct.

★ **Ask follow-up (open-ended) questions.**

★ **Limit drawing parallels from your own life into their story.**

★ **Avoid filling silence with your own words and interjections.**

PARENTING TRAP: relying on too many extrinsic motivators

The dangers of leasing teenage motivation: Sometimes consumers lease vehicles they can't afford to own. There is little (if any) down payment required and the monthly payment is certainly cheaper than a purchase; good credit, minimal paperwork and zoom, they're off. There they go, driving off in a new vehicle without saving for a down payment or creating the necessary room in their budget to actually purchase the car; it's quicker, cheaper, and initially easier than buying. But it can create a lease cycle difficult to shake; when the lease term ends a new lease must be assumed and the monthly payment never ceases. Though the lessee has made their payment each month, they are, in fact, no closer to owning the vehicle.

The same trap exists when parents lease motivation from their children: short term perks followed by a longer-term dilemma.

Examples of extrinsic motivators:

✓ Money for grades

✓ Cars for grades

✓ Trips with friends for grades

✓ Right to engage in adult behaviors for grades

Why parents do it: Frustrated parents are thirsty for a quick fix; waiting for teenage motivation to kick-in can be an exhausting process, and sometimes it's simply more satisfying to grab the *other shoe* by its strings rather than waiting for it to *drop*. But in the long run, leasing teenage motivation creates the same dilemmas found in any lease cycle: payments are made, but no real equity is gained. Over-incentivizing positive behaviors and outcomes from children initially produces gains, but inherently promotes a scenario where parents never cease paying for motivators.

So how do parents buy teenage motivation? You can't. You can, however, provide a motivational down payment in the form of shelter, food, education, and access to formative experiences. Ultimately though, the teenager must make their own monthly payments.

This is where is gets tricky.

Parents often find themselves thinking *I've given them this or that and yet they still don't* ... so the impatient parent begins to barter; they begin leasing motivation. The elementary child is guaranteed $5 for each good grade on their next report card. Leased. The young teen promises no more missing assignments if they can go to the birthday party. Leased. The high school teen guarantees an A in Economics if they can just stay out past curfew. Leased. The pragmatics of these perks are fine, if they are reversed in distribution and actuated as a bonus instead of a clause. Huh? Quality academic product, positive final outcomes, and safe behaviors should be standard, not attached to money, an event, or a curfew.

Leasing ideal behaviors and grades is temporarily rewarding, but promotes a false expectation that doing well warrants extrinsic rewards. It doesn't. Children must discover for themselves their internal degree of motivation, free from extrinsic motivators.

The instinctual reaction of any parent is to save their child, but it is critical to define what warrants a save. Drowning, save. Abusing substances, save. Posting unhealthy content online, save. Not completing every homework assignment, don't save. Not every sign of low motivation needs to be actively addressed.

Instead, analyze what percentage of your frustration stems from your teenager not being motivated versus them not having *your* motivation. Parents might want things for their children that those children don't want for themselves. As frustrating as it can be, stepping back and looking at life through their lens is important. This perspective will prevent you from trying to illicit behaviors and outcomes that only exist through leasing motivations, or in more simple terminology, bribes.

Patience and strategic intervention are two vital tools in the war on (lack of) motivation. Sometimes kids need to experience the real world and academic side effects of not making their payment. Without external (non-parental) forces holding them accountable they will never discover their own motivational voice. Motivational leasing techniques prevent children from honing intrinsic motivation.

Motivational leases create children who only produce positive behaviors or outcomes when they are attached to instant gratification. And as they grow older, the complexity and cost of such external motivators increase as they grow bored of last year's model.

PARENTING TRAP: providing your teenager their college experience in high school

Teenagers today are hungry for adult freedoms and experiences earlier and earlier. They crave tangibles representing status and access. Ride sharing apps, fake IDs, music festival wrist bands, throwing house parties; these are social capital. In the same way

I was given an allowance by my parents, many teens are provided an allowance in the form of social capital and access. The college experience delivered in advance; but like a payday advance loan, the high interest paid on the back-end will overwhelmingly outweigh the initial benefits. Adult situations granted prematurely are dangerous to our teens and damage their still-developing adolescent brains and dull their sense of drive toward the college experience.

Traditionally the allure of college is newfound freedom: both intellectually and more so, socially. But if parents produce and deliver experiences that are more advanced than the environment they are entering—college becomes unappealing as it is not a new experience. When I went to college I had significantly fewer rules and restrictions. Now many college freshmen are finding the opposite. They have more freedom at home than at college. Access to alcohol, access to luxury accommodations, access to free meals, access to excused absences in lieu of test-taking. All of this is in direct contradiction to the reality of colleges they enter. Colleges have non-negotiable consequences regarding alcohol and behavior, and higher standards regarding intellectual property and plagiarism. Professors are not interested in why they missed a class, or a test.

PARENTING TRAP: trying to control your teen's everyday friendships

Friendgineering: I worked with parents conducting due diligence for their child's inevitable transition from her small private school to a larger public school. The parents evaluated the variables and factors that could impact this change. Admittedly, their daughter had expressed zero concern over the matter; perhaps the change was too far away to seem real, or perhaps she simply didn't know what she didn't know, and plugged along in the spirit of *ignorance is bliss*. But life experience provided her parents with doppler-like radar that forecasted the predictably unpredictable reality of what awaited her.

Our meeting traversed the peaks and valleys of her new educational landscape, yet routinely circled back to the region of teenage social dynamics. It was here that we broached the topic of *friendgineering*. Say what?

Friendgineers seek to control their child's friendships, by pairing them with or keeping them from a specific peer (group). These actions are motivated by social hierarchy and void of cause. While born from good intentions (think babies and play-dates) some parents now sadly overemphasize who their kids "are" as opposed to who their kids are. These parents were aware of the landmines awaiting their daughter, but weren't willing to recklessly insulate her from or actively drive her towards a certain kind of peer. The parents refused to be friendgineers. Props to them.

Tips to help your teenager find new, more healthy and appropriate peers:

★ **Help your child find their thing:** Maybe it's a traditional sport, or a martial art, or painting, or theater, or working; whatever it is, providing your children ample opportunity to be around like-minded and equally busy peers helps them find their lane, their niche, their thing, which in turn builds confidence, creates structure, and develops responsibility, all of which are valuable traits.

★ **Respect and use the power of proximity:** The expression *show me your five closest friends, and I'll show you your future* (credit: Matt Bellace) is true to a fault. Teens morph into a combination of their friends. New friendships stem from new opportunities to find them, so provide new experiences, new teams, and new environments for your children to make connections. Kids hang out with who they're around the most, so if you want to change who they're with, change how, when, and where they spend their time. Social osmosis is real; use it to your advantage.

★ **Maintain channels of communication:** Provide your children, early and often, with the framework to be successful. Clarify your family expectations, rules, aspirations, and unconditional love for them. Eliminate ambiguity; nothing negatively impacts teen decision-making more than ambiguity. Your children need to know the limits, the consequences, and that you will be consistent in your delivery as parents. If you build a fence, they'll play in the yard. And when they don't, they're not surprised by your reactions.

★ **Monitor, but don't disrupt:** My wife and I have discovered that some of the most anxiety-riddled situations our oldest daughter has experienced, she was completely unaware of. Really, it was our own insecurities shining through, as we descended down the rabbit hole as if her make-up dance class was a combination of *Liv and Maddie* and *House of Cards*. We anxiously walked her in, and left her, and watched, and waited ... as she just danced, and smiled, and laughed. You get the point.

★ **Drastic times call for drastic measures:** Sometimes working from behind the scenes simply won't cut it. The fundamental role of a parent is to keep your child safe, and if someone or something is making them otherwise, never hesitate to get involved. As described earlier, the parent would not police the menial, but he would never hesitate to remove her from a dangerous scenario where her safety was being marginalized.

★ **A practical case study:** The most vibrant children come from the same general pedigree: they have found their lane, surround themselves by like-minded peers, possess a clear understanding of their family paradigm, and have parents who provide them with enough real estate to learn and grow without giving away the farm.

PARENTING TRAP: When parents mistake their children for friends

Many parents allow their teens to consume alcohol. Commonly, this is based on a skewed logic pattern that allowing said consumption will make the teen "better" at drinking alcohol in college. Some take it a step further by furnishing both the alcohol and venue to make consumption more accessible. A toolkit. Awesome, right? Not so much.

First, a question: what does that really mean, to be "better" at drinking? Others trade out the phrase "better" with "more equipped"; semantics aside, the disconnect in logic is palpable and dangerous. Being "better" at or "more-equipped" to consume alcohol as a teenager is never constructive when viewed through the lens of widely-accepted scientific research. Yes, in the short-sighted throes of managing teens it is no doubt easier to allow than disallow consumption: a trade-off made to avoid conflict, keep better tabs on children, and appear more "chill." Warning: this can and often does become a deal with the Devil.

The opposite approach, of not being an active participant in your teen's alcohol consumption, requires a steadfast commitment to avoid this "chill" parent phenomenon. It requires parents to zoom out and ask: how does "better" or "more-equipped" look long-term in the health and vibrancy of my teen? Hint: not well. Teenage brain development is restricted by alcohol. Long-term memory is adversely affected; alcohol fuels volatility and hostility, disrupts sleep patterns, and lends itself to depression and anxiety. Teens are significantly more likely to develop long -erm addictions and less likely to develop resiliency when alcohol enters their social regimens. When the relationship between alcohol and emotions is fostered, your child is stripped of their emotional framework to effectively withstand Hurricane Life. Teens need to experience and endure the full spectrum of emotions (happiness, sadness, disappointment, heartbreak) without the use of alcohol as a crutch.

Permissive drinking creates the illusion that its use is acceptable, expected, and necessary; none of these are true. Not to mention it is illegal! Imagine the convoluted message your permission sends: certain laws are negotiable; it's okay to ignore your health; and forget the long-term game. Do you furnish cigarettes or marijuana to your teens, encourage them to speed in their car, plagiarize essays or steal? I could go on. Still down to provide a keg and a basement for your teen and half of the local high school?

PARENTING TRAP: When parents over-insulate their teenager

As high schoolers enter their final years of living at home, many parents begin pumping the brakes on rules while increasing adult freedoms to better prepare them for the "real world." College is not the "real world." I would support this approach if your child was actually entering the "I'm an adult and I have bills to pay" world. Adult freedoms are for adults; they are warranted when the rent or mortgage is paid, full-time and gainful employment is held, and autonomous responsibility and financial accountability for said actions and mistakes are demonstrated.

Your child already lives in the real world; we all do. This is their phase in the real world, so should we willfully allow them to fast forward through it, or skirt it completely? As an adult and parent, it is well-known that time is precious, in a don't-blink invaluable sort of way; each phase of it is vital and necessary, although seemingly awkward or painful at times. Why speed up time in this short life we live? Just because 50 is the new 40 does not mean high school has to be the new college.

PARENTING TRAP: When parents give their teenagers a longer-than-healthy leash

Another innocent landmine is the belief that it is no longer necessary to assertively monitor the actions, whereabouts, and behaviors of your teen. Why? Older teens need more accountability and not less; it's a you-can't-put-lipstick-on-a-pig, kind of thing. Grey is not a color that teens wear well; they need black and white contrast. Do this, not that. If you do this, that happens. They crave clear lines. Older teenagers are more likely to engage in risky behaviors with more permanent consequences. Think DUI, think pregnancy, think medical marijuana cards and dealing drugs, think felony.

While I openly endorse assertive monitoring, I do recommend packaging it in such a way that eases conflict with your teen. Perhaps you create a contract. Or incentivize positive behaviors through earned freedoms. Whatever the case, be creative and collaborative. The short-term reality is that you will be so annoying, the worst parent, the uncool parent. However, this short-term cost is infinitely usurped by preventing potentially fatal errors and lapses in judgment that could leave you without a child to parent. Would you rather be uncool with a healthy child or cool without one?

PARENTING TRAP: When parents replace age-appropriate peers with teenagers

Mistakenly, many parents consider it timely and appropriate to begin transitioning from parent to friend while their children are still in high school. This well-intentioned act makes it increasingly difficult to assert control when the child views their parent as a peer. Directives from peers are purely optional advice. Your child has friends; you do not need to be one, at least not right now.

If you consider your teenager one of your best friends, please stop reading this and open Instagram or Facebook. Identify someone plus or minus five years of your age; that person is your friend. While you're at it, check out your teen's profile to see what they're up to. Your child is your child, you are their parent; if they want to be friends with you it's because they're playing you. Seriously, if you need friends, look towards your own peer group and go out and meet people. Join a tennis club or a book club, or take a cooking class; befriend the parents of your child's friends; do something. You, as a parent need and deserve a support system and outlet of your own! But it should not be vicariously through your own child.

Thirteen years ago, when my wife and I were new residents of Southern California, we knew no one so we joined a kickball league (I know, right?!); fast forward to present time ... they are still some of our closest friends. Our OGs.

Reset your practice, now: I urge you to collectively coral the booze; allow your teen to live in their true phase of life; create clear expectations and manage behaviors carefully; parent your teen; and do it all out of, and with, love.

Calibrating your family paradigm: One of the most important and impactful activities I do with families is guide them through the process of calibrating their family paradigm. Say what? This (albeit wordy) process flushes out and identifies areas within the family structure that lack clarity or consistency. In short: are both parents parenting from the same general parental zip code? The parents-teen, rules-expectations-reality game can and will quickly turn into a tangled web of chaos without all parties knowing exactly what's going on, and why.

This calibration process clarifies how conscious you, as parents, are of your own parenting. Do you have a plan? An end game? A moral compass guiding your rules? Or is it mainly a bunch of audibles and by-the-seat-of-the-pants moments woven together into a series of tense and inconsistent moments? The process exposes the degree to which (of lack thereof) your teen is aware of your rules. And more, why the rules exist at all. *My child most certainly knows the rules.* So you say. I know that sounds a bit harsh, but it's very common for parents to *think* they have made a rule or expectation clearly understood, when realistically it is completely lost on said teenager. More important, the process really drills down to the why behind your parenting. Why do they have to be home by ten? Why can't they shotgun beers at concerts? Being able to articulate a clear value-based why is far more powerful than simply shouting one of my personal favorites *because I said so.* Does this mean every executive parenting decision warrants or calls for an elaborate values-driven rationale? Certainly not.

Many parents hold on to an idealistic fantasy in which they confuse (subconsciously) the rules and expectations that they would like to implement, maintain, and enforce, with the rules and expectations that they implement, maintain, and enforce. On paper they look assertive, clear and comprehensive, but in real life, no so much. I remember when my wife and I were new parents, we held onto certain idealistic notions of what kind of parents we were going to be; *We're going to read to her every day, twice per day.* But soon, covered in poop and taunted by sleep deprivation, we discovered it was much easier to say and exponentially harder to do (*reads once per day, every other day; mostly*).

Ask yourself these kinds of questions to clarify your paradigm:

✓What are your non-negotiables regarding your children?

✓What are the actions/behaviors that are 100% unacceptable in your household?

✓What is the bottom shelf of acceptability for grades?

✓What is the college expectation you have for your children?

✓In five years from this moment … where do you want your teenager to be? Doing?

✓If there's only one quality you hope to instill in your teenager, it's ….

Being a proactive communicator: The sweat equity of being a proactive communicator with your children will save you many a conflict. Now that's not to say if you take the time as parents to thoughtfully decide on your core values and apply rules based on those, that your teen won't give you a run for you money; they will. The difference between the thoughtfully prepared you and the gunning-from-the-hip parents is the response to said envelope pushing. If you already know how you'll respond, and more important, why you'll respond that way, you are far more likely to be taken seriously both in the expediency of your reaction and the validity of your parental response.

Without a clearly defined, written or stated, family constitution (minus the cursive and waaaay shorter), you as a parent unit are heading into a game of poker that you cannot win. Or maybe you win occasionally; but still, playing poker is for weekends in a garage, or in Vegas on a couple's getaway, not in your living room with a teenager who's come home wasted (again).

In establishing a couple of *truths* to hold *self-evident* you save yourself the turmoil caused by making too many emotional, from-the-hip decisions. Those kinds of decisions are less effective (for one, you most likely won't actually do all you yelled you would) and those decisions tend to vary in severity based on your mood. It's about getting away from the trap of reaction and getting ahead.

It's about being proactive. By drilling down and establishing a couple of non-negotiables, with (mostly) automatic and consistent responses, you effectively lift the curtain of ambiguity and chop off the legs of wiggle room. Teeagers don't see grey; they need black and white.

Ambiguity is the enemy here; if your teenager does not know how you will react, they will test and see what kind of reaction they get this time. They will hedge their bet, raise you, call your bluff and see if or how often you hold. Worst of all? They're playing with house (your) money. Take back control.

The semantics Olympics: Parenting in its most organic, fluid, and commonly unorganized state of being, can be efficiently and alarmingly mirrored with the classic Abbott and Costello bit, *Who's on First*. The sketch, albeit from the 30s, is uncomfortably similar to the layers of linguistic convolution parents experience when managing teenagers. *Who's on First* strikes a chord not only with its accuracy regarding the compounding effect that clarity, and lack of clarity, reap on basic human communication and understanding, but also in that it so perfectly demonstrates how even a tiny bit of initial miscommunication can kick the can-of-miscommunication miles down the road.

Unfamiliar with the bit? Let's take a closer look
for comparison's sake.

Costello: Then who gets it?

Abbott: Naturally.

Costello: Naturally.

Abbott: Now you've got it.

Costello: I throw the ball to Naturally.

Abbott: You don't! You throw it to Who!

Costello: Naturally.

Abbott: Well, that's it—say it that way.

Costello: That's what I said.

Abbott: You did not.

Costello: I said I throw the ball to Naturally.

Abbott: You don't! You throw it to Who!

Costello: Naturally.

Mom: Then where are you going?

Son: Josh's.

Mom: Josh's.

Son: Now you've got it.

Mom: So you're going to Josh's.

Son: No; I'm going to Jake's!

Mom: Jake's.

Son: Well, that's it—say it that way.

Mom: That's what I said.

Son: You did not.

Mom: I said you're going to Jakes's.

Son: No, I'm not; I'm going to Josh's!

Mom: Josh's.

Now repeat this conversation, within the context of just about every area of parent-son communication and you're left with nothing short of a hair-pulling-worthy cycle of living under one roof, but existing on two entirely different pages.

So, what's an Abbot supposed to do with their teenage Costello?

One extremely effective cadence for successfully managing teenage behaviors can be broken down into four parts:

1) **Clarify.**
2) **Solidify.**
3) **Memorialize.**
4) **Enforce.**

1) Clarify: Clarity is vital because parents typically have two sets of rules: the ones they think they have, and the ones they really have. The first step is sitting down as a parental unit and determining what are the (actual) rules? Actual rules. Not the ones in dream-land. But what are the rules you have in play right now. For example, if your curfew is 11:00 p.m. on weekends, but your 10th grader has gone unscathed for the past six months when ducking in at 11:45 p.m. ... then your curfew is 11:45 p.m. Which leads me to my next key point for consideration: who knows the rules? To make my point, let's beat my last example over the head a few more times. If your 10th grader is home at 11:45 p.m. and you are still holding out hope that your curfew is 11:00 p.m., that beckons the question: is it that they know the curfew and are ignoring you and exploiting your failure to enforce said rule? Or is it that you are assuming they know, and they really don't.

The next step in this soul-searching is to evaluate why those rules exist. A rule without meaning behind it is invalid; kids see right through them; they're a pain in the ass to enforce. So, it's critical to make sure that your rules (and this is why you need to avoid having too many rules) are attached to your core values. Core values are easy to defend, as they hold true meaning to your being, and who you are, or want to be known, as a family. When you stand your ground based on a moral compass, the pure anger which spews from the angry eyes of a mad-as-hell teen is easier to manage.

2) Solidify: Imagine for a minute that your parenting structure is the frame of a house. It's nicely appointed, painted, complete with doors, double-pane windows and a shingled roof to keep the rain out. Regardless of how your homes shows from the curb, in reality, it is really only as strong as the foundation it rests upon. In parenting we get caught up and spend lots of parental energy and emotion focusing on the whats. *What party can I go to? What time do I need to come home? What will happen if I don't?* And so on. Don't get me wrong, whats are great. I love whats; they are very important in running a tight ship; but they hold little meaning without a solid why to support them. Keep it simple. Creating too many rules increases the likelihood of having unenforced rules, and unenforced rules is worse than having no rules. Thus, it's important to only pick a few key rules that support your family value system. These rules should be broad enough, and flexible enough to avoid the parent being backed into a corner. *Nobody backs Baby into a corner...* unless Baby is the name of a parent with an extraordinarily long and overly detailed list of rules. Just make sure your rules cover the bases and anticipate the teenage envelope-pushing (and envelope crumpling, ripping up, etc.) of a self-finding teen.

3) Memorialize: I like parent-teen contracts as much as I dislike them. You'll notice a theme here. I think they're wonderful if and when they are properly utilized. Much like the Texas Hold 'Em approach to parenting, the biggest mistake that parents make when using a contract with their teen, is using the contract as a starting point in the negotiating process. If you haven't picked up on it by now, I do not suggest negotiating with a teenager; they have way more to gain than their parents, and far less to lose. Contracts that are presented in a top-downy manner are less likely to establish a foothold of buy-in or acceptance from a teenager.

One tool vital to more streamlined and better understood family expectations is regularly scheduled and held family meetings. Family meetings that are consistent allow the teenager and parent alike to know that there is an appropriate, expected, and valid platform for them to air their grievances and present their case for whatever issue is at hand. I realize I just got done telling you not to negotiate with teens, but healthy and engaged dialogue is different than negotiating. Garnering their feedback, perspective, and input will allow you to make more aware parenting choices, with a stronger understanding of their self-described wants and needs. This does not mean that you placate them, but it will allow you to more confidently make parenting choices, and stand in those decisions with more authentic strength and fortitude.

The objective of the initial family meeting is to memorialize your teen's understanding of the family rules and consequences. This doesn't mean that they will agree with them or even like them; but the purpose is to create the fence, the black and white, the cans and cannots. Certainly there different levels of understanding and degrees to which that agreement of understanding will change. The family meeting should be short, polite, and routine; a one-and-one meeting every six months is not effective. One reason for the ineffective quality of a *once-in-a-blue-moon* family meeting is that typically they are only motivated by negative behaviors. If the only time you meet with your teenagers is to read them their rights and lay out punishment, they'll further avoid any and all communication with you. Regular family meetings also make time for the much needed, yet overlooked, lowkey acknowledgement of your teen's accomplishments and positive actions. We live in an assembly-heavy society: lots of pomp and certificates. That is fine; but more regular reinforcement of what you appreciate about, or are prideful about, in regard to your teenager's daily life, will yield a higher probability of those behaviors and actions. Teenagers are in many ways little kids in big bodies, so it's okay to lay it on thick sometimes.

4) Enforce: Ah, yes. Follow through. Easy to do when they're little. Remember when they would have timeout? And stay in timeout? Sure, some small children can be pretty combative at times, but not to the degree teens will let you have it. So for many parents, enforcing rules is way easier not to do. For one thing, it is perfect for avoiding conflict. Follow-through and rule-enforcement is energetically taxing as well as seemingly fruitless. This is where it is key to remember that your follow-through and enforcement on the small stuff significantly decreases the odds of there being big stuff (or as much of it) as they grow older.

The primary reason that enforcement is so challenging for parents of teenagers is that they have not adequately thought through their parental plan of action. There has not been proper mental energy and parent-to-parent dialogue allocated to planning ahead. As I have already touched on, a large majority of parents suffer from either *not my kid* or *I used to do that, too*; both of which are great tactics for waiting for something much worse to happen. And failing to plan ahead, or resting on the laurels of denial is not a strategy of assertive parents. Again, all the suggestions and insight I have been laying out in this text needs to be put through the filter of your family paradigm. I don't recommend having hundreds of rules and spending long afternoons identifying infractions and being a dictator within the castle. I do, however, want to remind you that if you do not enforce rules when the infraction is low voltage, you might just get electrocuted by a strong current of what-the-eff-did-my-teen-just-do in the not so distant future. So, yeah, if you make a rule, and they break it, some parental acknowledgement is required.

PARENTING TRAP: when your career usurps your ability to be an engaged parent

Perhaps this is you, or your spouse ... there you are, a paragon of success. Gainfully employed. Grinding through a career and well-appointed reality. Bumpin' to some early Nelly in your luxury-grade vehicle, you assertively navigate the hustle-and-flow, collecting promotions, bonuses, while assuming ever-increasing responsibility. A family-focused parent, you're a loving and loyal person with beautiful children and an enviable life. The catch? This life has overhead: sweat equity in the form of sacrifice. Collateral damage in the form of an alienated teenager. The kicker? The alienation was abrupt, lacked warning, and feels impenetrable. The good news: that awesome description of you above. The bad news: unless you make some adjustments, the alienation that feels impenetrable, will, in fact, become impenetrable.

Tips to help restore, reinforce, or repair a strained busy-professional parent and teen relationship:

★ **Carve out (scheduled) time with your teen:** Take a moment to look at the calendar on your iPhone. Of the appointments, how many, if any, are with your teen? And if so, how many are obligatory (sports, doctor, dentist, DMV, court)? Any left? While teenagers don't require *much* individual attention from parents, they *do* require it. Teens need routine face time with their parents. Regardless of what it looks like, the most crucial tenet is frequency. Establishing a routine will benefit all parties; it will become normal amidst the layers of your busy world. So, dive in, pick a day and time, and commit to spending it with your teenager. No, passing in the hallway, or on the driveway or freeway doesn't count. And neither does a group setting; one-on-one is best. Start simple: drive them to school; bring lunch and eat together in your car; play 9 holes on a par 3. Anything is better than nothing, assuming it's just you, and its routine. The *what* matters far less than the *why*. Spending time with your teenager will provide them with positive validation and prevent negative attention-seeking behaviors.

★ **Establish an open line of communication via text and social media:** Your teenager annoys you with their heavy phone use; they're always on it, it's glued to them, *blah, blah, blah*. But zoom out and you'll discover it provides a sense of connection. And if you can't beat 'em, join 'em. Speak your teen's language by engaging via their #nextgen platforms. Send entertaining, and nag-free links, memes, or messages during the week. Follow them on social media. Create a fantasy football league to capitalize on passion and increase causal correspondence. Form a group chat for your entire family to quickly and informally check-in. Whatever it is, keep it light and positive to foster and repair your relationship. Avoid lecturing, over-reminding, and nagging at all costs. The sum of these causal interactions will make the difficult ones accessible, so be strategic in your approach.

★ **Wrap your head around the academics of high school:** It's imperative to know the details about your teen's high school academics. And while sports are awesome, there's more to the picture. Many functional ways exist to keep you *in the loop*. Most schools use web-based, iPhone-friendly grading platforms, complete with a downloadable app, giving you access to all pertinent information. Too often career-focused parents shift these access points out of their primary awareness. And while you don't need to know every detail, you should maintain enough insight to facilitate a guided conversation when the need arises. If you open each school-related discussion by needing a reminder of courses and teacher names, your teen will use this to keep you at bay. A stark difference exists between a conversation with a well-informed parent, who is asking specific questions, and one being reminded of basic details (for the fifth time). Finally, when a school conference is required, attend; the most effective parents operate well by being authentically informed and engaged.

★ **Parlay high school requirements into bonding activities:** Many high schools have a community service requirement; and all colleges view service-learning with high regard. In the spirit of killing two birds with one stone, volunteer alongside your teenager in these obligations. By rolling up your sleeves and joining in, you get a chance to see your child through a new lens by watching them interface with elderly adults at a senior center, veterans at the VA hospital, impoverished families at a soup kitchen, or other cultures on a mission trip. Regardless of the scope, these comfort-zone pushing scenarios create an element of discomfort in teens, pulling them closer to you (much like a toddler at a dinner party). Or perhaps they will shock you with their gregarious personality and engaging persona. As a bonus, they see your skills normally reserved for work, like social swagger, confident delegation, multi-tasking and brute strength. In all, you both win; your teenager doesn't have to complete hours alone, and a bonding opportunity, if only from osmosis and proximity, is born.

★ **Revive the family meal:** The family that eats together, sticks together. It's another effective strategy is spending time together within the greater family unit. Pull the patriarch card and round up the herd to sit down and have a weekly meal. Pick a meal, any meal, but as reiterated, be consistent. Realistically speaking, schedules vary, so remain flexible, but don't skip the weekly meal. A few ground rules: include all members of the clan, no iPhones, no iPads, no TV on the flat screen, and no leaving early. Couple those with: no mention of work, or school, no lectures, no nit-picking and no overly boastful trips down memory lane. What should you expect? Well at first, expect long stretches of awkward silence and dish-clinging. And you'll certainly notice the absence of everything that served as a comfort blanket. The devices and conversation staples were minutia; they said and contributed nothing substantive toward family bonding. But over time, the weekly meal will become enjoyable, a welcomed departure from your face-paced lives, and a chance to stay connected, in a life that has you neatly compartmentalized into various stages of life.

Moving Forward

Here we are. The end of our time together. My hope is that *The Assertive Parent* has better equipped and inspired you to engage with teenagers with equal parts optimism and pragmatic reality. We have thoroughly examined the various parenting norms that may have (at times) manipulated or stunted your intuitive parenting philosophies and practices. We've reflected common parenting traps—whether inconsistency, ignorance or sheer exhaustion. We've revisited the headache and heartaches brought forth either by the poor decisions or mistakes your teenager, or ones incurred against them by others. It's imperative to remember that parenting teenagers an ever-changing, tall order—and the only fatal mistake, is to give up efforts it takes to curate authentically autonomous young adults.

There is no magic formula to be a perfect parent and there should be no expectations that teenagers will walk this life void of significant challenges in the character, confidence and motivation departments. Regardless of what's happened in the past, the final pages of this book bring opportunity to recalibrate and start anew, with a more clarified vision for your intentions and focus moving forward—armed with new hacks, strategies and awareness that if used, will make your path toward being a more successful parent more viable. But as the saying goes, the fortune is in the follow through. Keep this book at arm's length, next to the bed, or in the car, or at your desk—and use it, frequently.

Writing this book was difficult for me at times. On the most basic level, I love teenagers, they're some of my favorite humans—armed with optimism, self-assumed invincibility and typically a love for life (at least the parts of it that they enjoy). And by calling them out, so to speak, by drawing attention to their common teenage tendencies, was done purely out of love, not judgement. Equally challenging, was wading into the murky waters of haphazard parenting techniques that I have seen fail time and again. These anecdotes, just like the ones regarding teens, are written from a place of love, not judgement.

Teenagers often lack the proper confidence, moral framework, formative life experiences and internal decision-making systems to live their best, most authentic lives. We adults must create and foster an environment rich in morality, ethics, structure, consistency and forgiveness. Teenagers, more than kids in any other age or stage, need the framework of support and accountability, love and validation, to reach their full capacity. In fact, they crave these. As such, I encourage you to comb through the hundreds of options, anecdotes, and strategies in this book to amplify and fortify the requisite environment to help the teenagers in your lives attain the most authentic version of themselves. I challenge you to capture any negative, fearful, regretful or remorseful emotions circulating in your being, and convert them into the much-needed fuel that will allow you to optimize the privilege of parenting your children. Teenagers are truly inspirational beings who can, and will, rise to the occasion when given the opportunity to be heard, feel included, live their truth and be held accountable for their poor choices, while meaningfully praised and supported during times of authentic success.

In approaching your parenting from this point forward, there's no perfect way to begin—begin *wherever* you can, *however* you can, within the framework of your life.

I leave you with eight steps as you launch:

★ **Be reflective:** take a hard look at your parenting. Good, bad, ugly. All of it. Honesty is the biggest ally to progress. Examine your systems, habits, significant strengths, mistakes, potential improvements. When you get clear with your past, the future will assume the identity aligned with your new goals.

★ **Journal:** write down everything you seek to accomplish in your parenting. This is not to be confused with writing a list of attributes and accomplishments that you want for your teen. What do you want to implement, change, or improve? By when? How? Set goals. Be ambitious. Go big! Keep track of your journey, feelings, reactions, successes, missteps along the way—thereby building a real-time and reflective roadmap from which to navigate next steps. Pen to paper is a powerful and completely underutilized source of lasting success.

★ **Show excuses the door:** excuses do little for anyone, anytime. They absolve you from accountability and distract your efforts to identify the true root causes that manifest in parent-teenage drama. Excuses and extenuating circumstances are different. Things happen, many out of your control, and that's okay. But make a conscious choice not to malign your parenting potential by assigning a "reason" to every negative decision, interaction, or situation that arises.

★ **Forget the fear:** you can still be afraid of bears, and bees, and the dark—but teenagers, no longer. Fearing the work, pain, tears, and stress of assertively parenting your teenager as their own unique human being is a choice. Forget the parenting choices everyone around you is making, or who you thought your child would be (versus who they really are) and focus fiercely on loving your teenager in their present state—concurrent with your courageous efforts of helping them reach their God-given capacity. Communication, confrontation, tough-love, and structure are all discomforts that must become viewed through a lens of love, not fear. Replace the fear with love, and you will be fine.

★ **Communicate early and often:** never assume that anyone in your life knows what you are feeling or thinking, particularly your teenagers. Communication channels with teenagers can close based on two basic factors: overuse or nonuse. Split the difference. Learn to maintain channels with your teen, using the techniques outlined throughout this book, so you don't find yourself in complete communicative isolation.

★ **Hold yourself accountable:** much of this book is about holding teenagers accountable—but they are only half of the puzzle. Establish ways to hold yourself accountable to the changes, strategies, interventions, and personal lifestyle choices, etc., that you have committed to implement. An easy place to begin is within this book (and if you haven't filled it out yet, that's the first place to start). Find a confidante, perhaps it's a spouse, a sibling, or a close friend, to meet with or call weekly as a formal check-in. Share your goals—own them, be proud of them. Draft timelines, establish due dates, and add reminders in your phone. Parenting teenagers is not a perfection game, it's a progress game, and having an ac-countability partner will ease the burden of going it alone.

★ **Keep swimming upstream:** tune in and listen to your internal moral compass. Put social, carpool, happy hour, lunch date, and co-worker "earplugs" in and walk your truth—parent to *your* vision. Chase your goals. In the short term, it will always be a more leisurely ride if you follow the strong current of trendy, enablement-reliant, blind-eye-loving parenting. Don't do it. Be courageous. Get exhausted. The longer you swim upstream, the stronger you'll become; when your child is an adult, they will thank you—with autonomy, financial independence, a college admission that matches their soul, and a career, *and life*, where they are completely fulfilled.

For more resources please visit
www.pattersonperspective.com

4/22 10-2 pm
BBC Open
interview